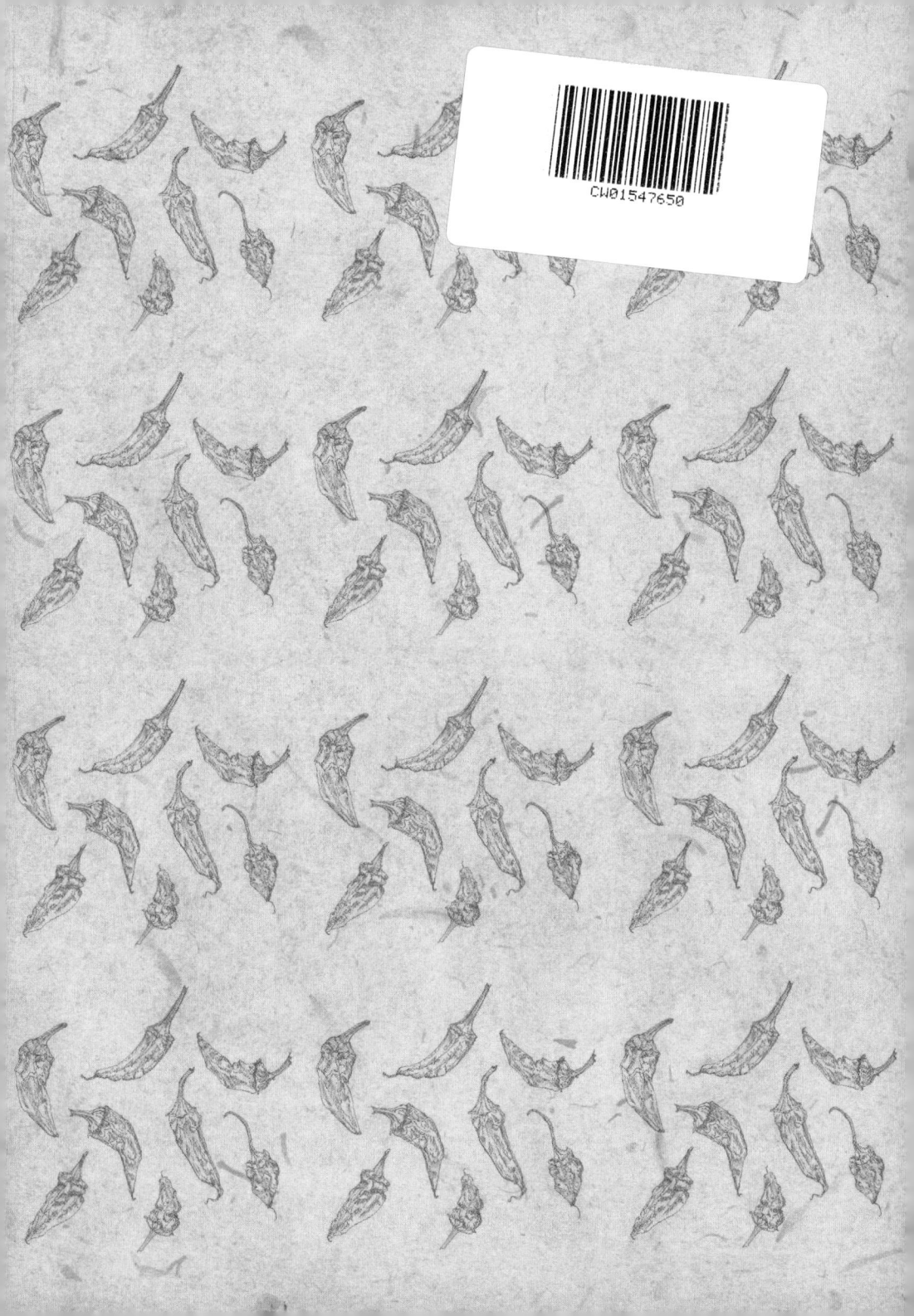

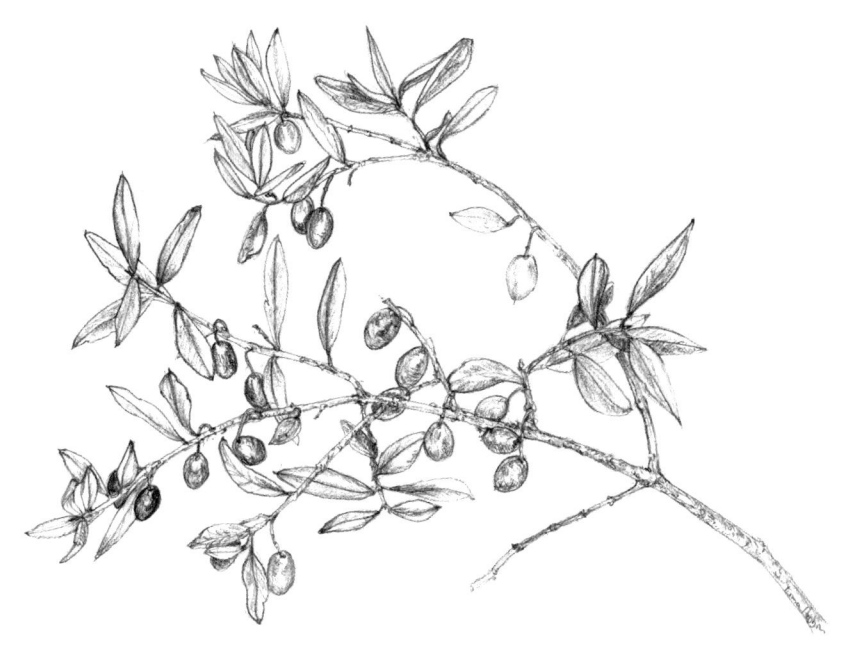

UNDER
THE OLIVE TREE

First published by Unicorn
an imprint of Unicorn Publishing Group LLP, 2020
5 Newburgh Street
London W1F 7RG
www.unicornpublishing.org

Text © Anna Maggio, 2020
Illustrations © Emma Hobbins, 2020

All rights reserved. No part of the contents of this book may
be reproduced, stored in or introduced into a retrieval system,
or transmitted, in any form or by any means (electronic,
mechanical, photocopying, recording or otherwise), without the
prior written permission of the copyright holder and the above
publisher of this book.

Every effort has been made to trace copyright holders and
to obtain their permission for the use of copyright material.
The publisher apologises for any errors or omissions and
would be grateful if notified of any corrections that should be
incorporated in future reprints or editions of this book.

ISBN 978-1-913491-08-6
10 9 8 7 6 5 4 3 2 1

Designed by Emma Hobbins and Felicity Price-Smith
Printed in Europe on behalf of Latitude Press Ltd

UNDER THE OLIVE TREE

memories and flavours
of
Puglia

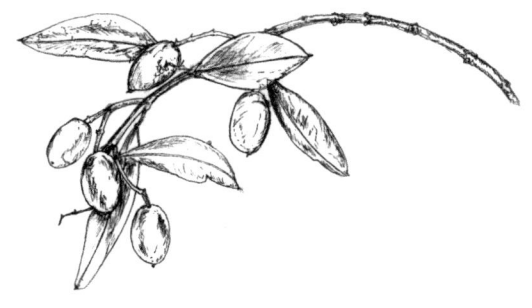

by

Anna Maggio

Illustrated by Emma Hobbins

UNICORN

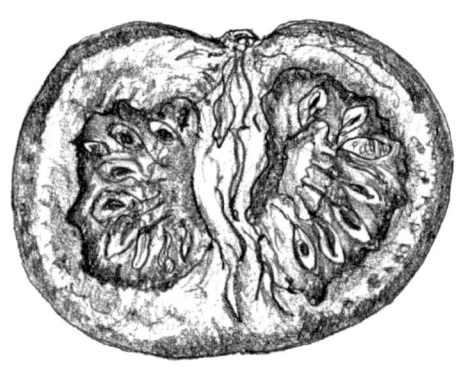

*This book is dedicated to my mother,
to Puglia and to the simple pleasures in life.*

Contents

Endings and Beginnings   6

From Puglia to East Sheen and back again   10

The magic of Puglia   15

Antipasti • Starters   16

The Seasons of Puglia   21

Primavera • Spring   22

Estate • Summer   37

Autunno • Autumn   50

Inverno • Winter   68

Pesce • Fish   84

Un po' di questo e quello • A bit of this and that   94

List of recipes in page order   107

Endings and Beginnings

Sitting at the kitchen table and sipping my first cup of coffee in the morning gives me a moment of stillness and reflection. I gaze at my garden, and the urge to rush out and check whether there is a palpable difference since yesterday fills me with expectations and dreams. In such quiet moments, I can find myself taken back to myriad memories or forward to hopes and fantasies. Images of my childhood arrive in my mind and I often ask myself what was it like being born in Trinitapoli, Puglia, just after the war.

When I ponder the past, I remember T.S. Eliot's words *'memories draped by the beneficent spider'*. What to include and what to leave out? My mother, who became a widow when I was only a year old, had to keep my brother and me fed and clothed by cooking at all hours of the day and night for the *signori,* the gentry of the land. She had to be strong and practical and, as her amazing skills in the kitchen were much sought after, we children were the lucky receivers of delectable morsels left by the paying signori. When food was plentiful, we were happy.

From the happy poverty of Puglia to affluent Milano – the exodus to the promised land. We arrived there in 1956 with our few belongings packed in cardboard boxes (just like Visconti's *Rocco e i suoi fratelli)*. Our accents gave away our origin: we were the *terroni* from the South and were treated like unwelcome immigrants.

I was not prepared for the coldness of the Milanese people and its climate, nor its insipid food. Suddenly there were no friends or neighbours around, and my mother disappeared early in the morning, working to pay the rent and put food on the table.

This was not Trinitapoli, and I was a 10 year old girl feeling quite lost in the big city, with nobody to talk to and nowhere to go except to school.

From an early age, my thirst for learning, the arts, music and the workings of the mind, made me question why we are here. University was not an option – I started working at 14 – but I read feverishly, and the millions of words that filled my mind gave me a hope that my world could be different. I had a fervent curiosity for the new, the untried.

I am a dreamer and always have been. In my dreams I always seek another way, another journey, another possibility waiting around the corner. I love to catch a moment, a phrase that fires my imagination before it slips away.

As a young woman I dreamt of thrilling new adventures and sparkling city lights, and in the late 60s I escaped the constrictions of the family and came to London with a married lover. It was like being plunged into another world. Nothing had prepared me for the aloofness and formality. Simply brushing against somebody's arm on a bus was something audacious and unwelcome. I soon learnt to say sorry. Conviviality was not on offer. Beans on toast were.

Food was not celebrated, and the shops selling fruit and vegetables made my heart ache: no plump ripe tomatoes, glistening peppers or soft juicy pears. I yearned for the markets of Puglia with all their vibrancy. But I was young and dreaming of liberty, love and excitement – all freely available in the swinging sixties – so I stayed and made London my home.

Living in the UK, and raising my 'half English' children, has meant that some Pugliese traditions have been lost, and increasingly I feel the urge to reconnect with myself as a young child, when I was happy with simple things. To revisit the land of my childhood and smell and savour again those intense flavours: a chunk of bread dipped in the juices of quickly fried olives just picked from the tree.

Puglia is a land where nature is unspoilt and culinary traditions are still very much alive. Sharing a bruschetta and a glass of wine can be more convivial than a banquet. This is what I now celebrate in a world increasingly devoid of unpretentious pleasures.

Memories and food are closely linked, entwining themselves in our consciousness. This book contains some of the recipes I have never forgotten: simple dishes invented with ingenuity to satisfy hunger, without losing sight of the enjoyment of food.

I often cook for my two grandchildren, Arthur and Rex, and I try to instill in them the pleasure we can get from simple food cooked with love. For me, food is never just a matter of sustenance; sharing food that has been prepared with care and love satisfies not just hunger but all the senses. There is invariably a sense of anticipation as we sit down *a tavola* to eat. Here is the place for animated discussions, for gossip, for family, for laughter and – why not? – for tears.

I used to watch my mother Isabella cooking in our tiny kitchen. She prepared dishes without any effort but with the knowledge that had been imparted to her by her mother, Anna, a fruit and vegetable seller in the local market. My mother was a truly instinctive cook – her energy in producing both elaborate and simple dishes seemed inextinguishable.

> *'We all live in exile, which is why we invented heaven.'*
> Germaine Greer, in a personal card

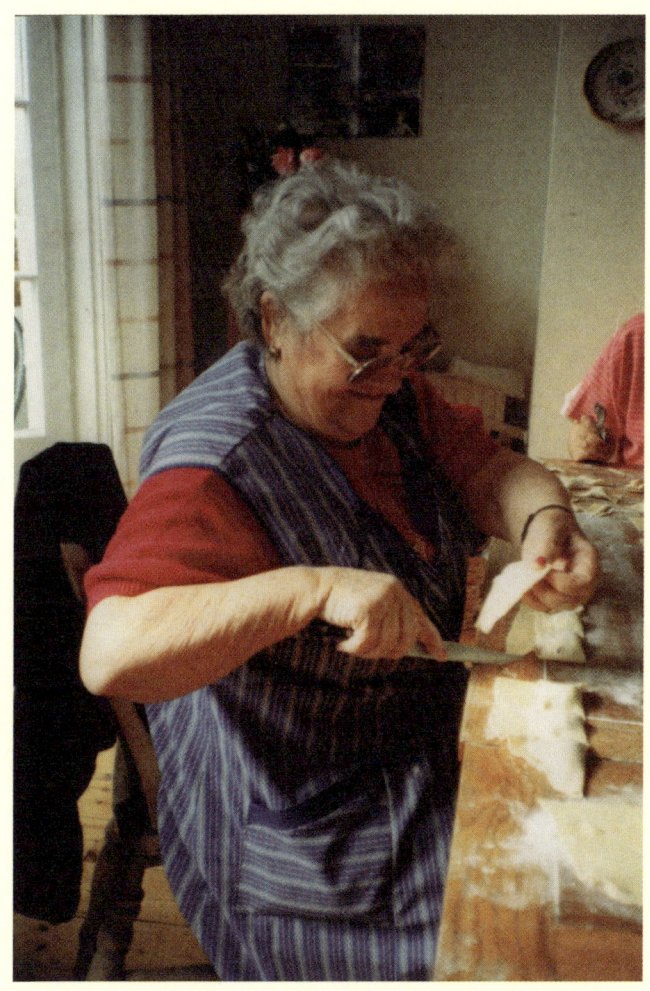

My mother Isabella in London

From Puglia to East Sheen and back again...

In a time of exile and displacement, it takes courage to travel back to where one started the journey of living.

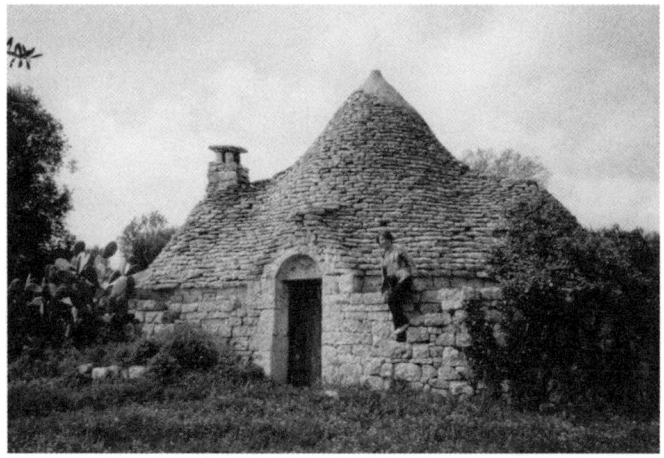

Twelve years ago, I bought a dilapidated 250 year old trullo with four acres of land in Pascarosa, near Ostuni in Puglia. Living in a world of frantic demands, I was in search of a place where I could exist for myself alone.

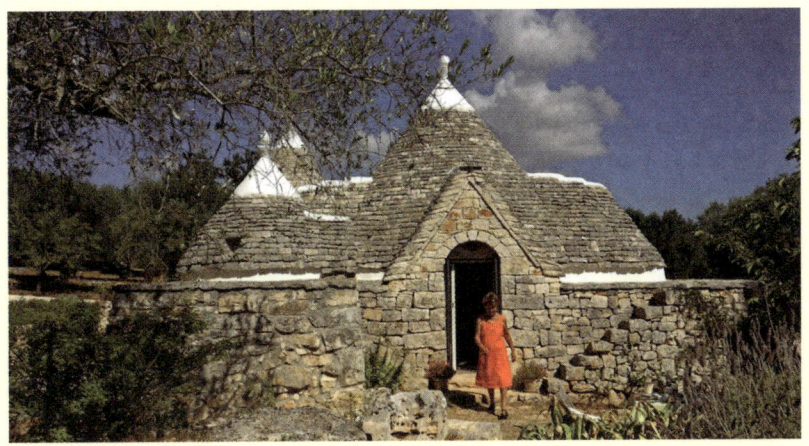

The renovation took its toll, but I now have a beautiful retreat where I can find my oasis of peace. Furthermore, when I arrive at Pascarosa, I am thrilled to be welcomed by trees in blossom or laden with the offerings of the season: olives, almonds, cherries, figs, plums, pears, quinces, pomegranates, walnuts, prickly pears, chestnuts, medlars, loquats – just some of the delights that grow in this fertile land.

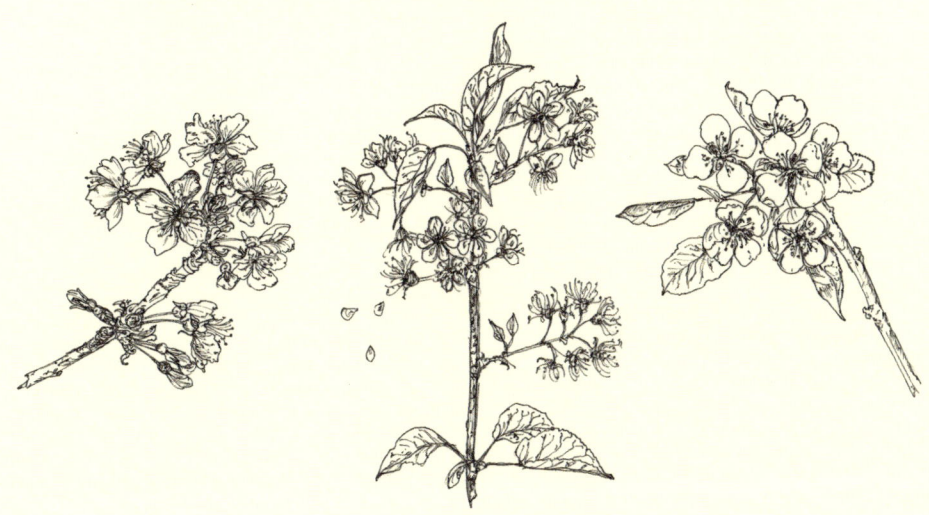

Although my life is not tied to the rhythms of nature, the fact that every crop is of short duration promotes a desire to make the best of it at the time, while conserving some for future use. Whenever I am at Pascarosa, I passionately gather, chop, boil, and fill jars with as many fruits as possible for my family and friends. It is a way of prolonging their survival.

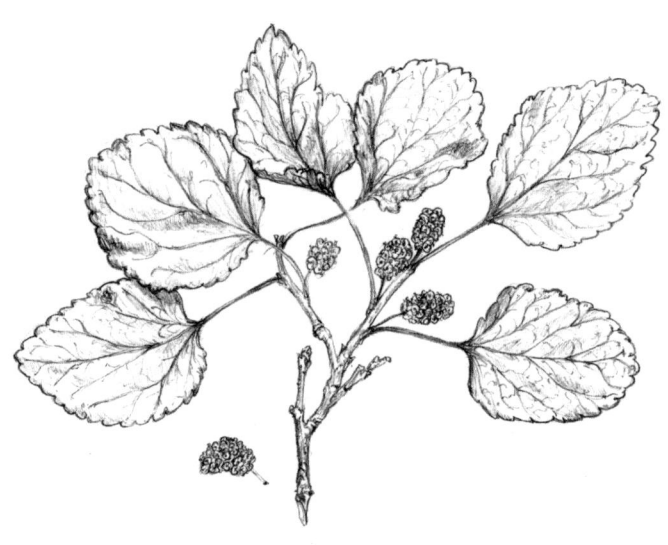

White mulberries at Pascarosa 29th June

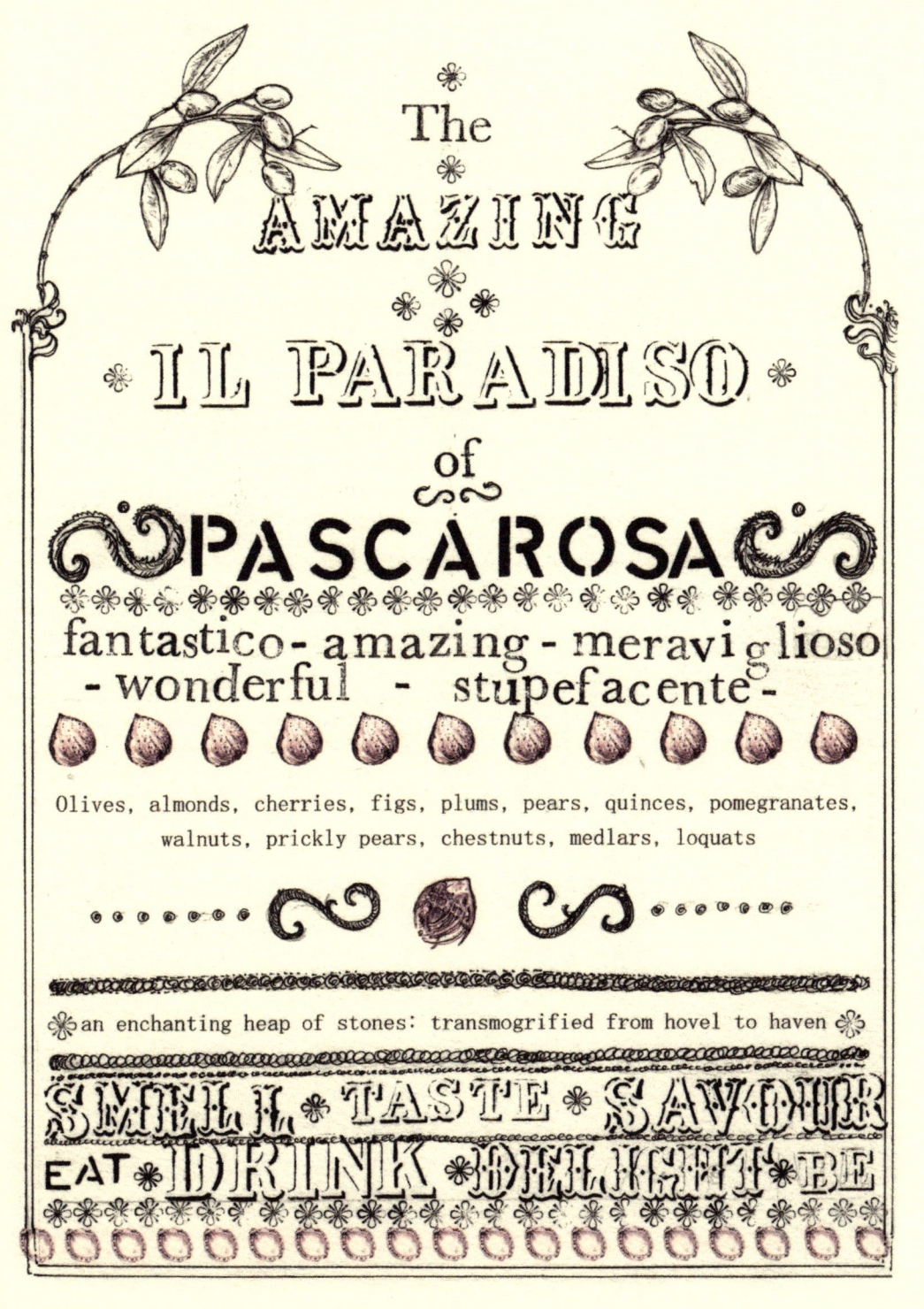

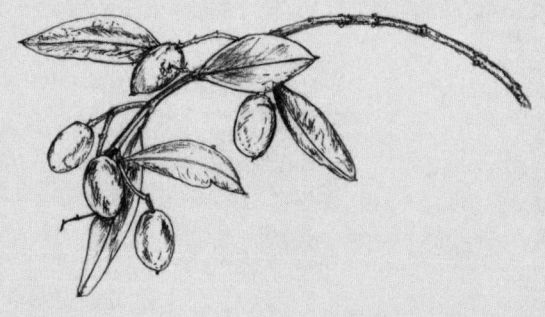

The Magic of Puglia Past and Present

Puglia is known as the *Mezzogiorno*, the land of eternal midday, where time slows down and nothing changes. It evokes images of an ancient past and distant peoples: Greeks, Arabs, Normans and Spaniards. They all left a legacy, a blend of traditions, folklore and religion. These influences have made Pugliese cuisine one of the most varied in the whole of Italy.

Above all, Pugliese people have kept their traditions going. The activities of preserving vegetables, drying tomatoes in the sun, and making passata for the winter months, are still very much part of our everyday life. My mother set aside the first week in August, when the tomatoes were ripe, to dedicate herself to this task: all of us children had to help with chopping, drying, boiling and sieving. There is something so evocative about the perfume of basil and the inebriating aromas of roasted peppers and *polpette* (meat balls) which I used to feed my children, Elisa and Simon every Thursday evening, when they came back, totally ravenous, from their swimming lesson.

Our simple, but nourishing diet has sustained us for centuries. We had no name for it: now it is fashionably called the 'Mediterranean diet'.

All of the following recipes serve 4, unless stated.

Antipasti

Our natural impatience and foraging habits dictate that, whilst waiting for the meal to be ready, we delight ourselves with tempting morsels, some in season, some that have been preserved for lean days. Pugliese antipasti are unique and a meal in themselves.

How can one refuse hot grilled aubergines soaked in fresh olive oil, juicy garlic and parmesan, a plate of tempting preserves (*sott'aceti*) such as *pomodori sott'olio* (the real sun-dried tomatoes!), *lambascioni* (bitter bulbs boiled and preserved in vinegar), or the crispy courgette flowers that go so well with a chilled glass of Locorotondo? Why not give in to the temptation of *cozze arraganate* (mussels)? Absolutely irresistible.

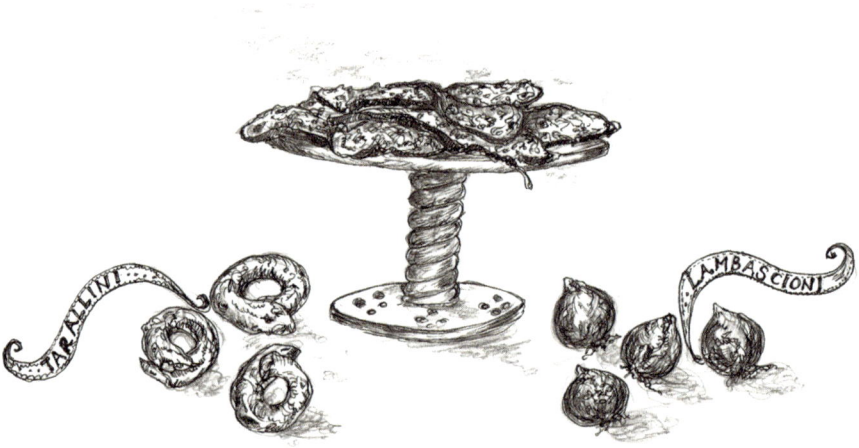

Bruschette originate from this ancient way of satisfying the hunger of the *contadini* (country people) during their lunch break, which had to be at midday precisely. *Frise* or *frisedde* (hard bread) would be soaked briefly in water and anointed with olive oil and crushed tomato, oregano and garlic. Delightful as a snack at any time.

Melanzane alla griglia
Grilled aubergines

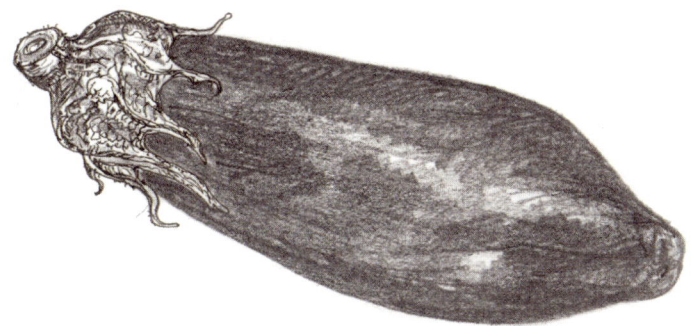

3 medium-sized aubergines
2 cloves of garlic, finely chopped
2 tbsp parsley, chopped
2 tbsp grated parmesan or pecorino cheese
extra virgin olive oil
salt and pepper

Slice the aubergines thinly lengthways, lay them on an oven tray and make some criss-cross incisions on each. Sprinkle with fine salt, brush with olive oil and cook in a hot oven for 10 minutes, turning the slices once. Remove from the oven and top the slices with chopped garlic, parsley, pepper, grated cheese and plenty of olive oil. Place them under the grill for 5 to 10 minutes or until the top is golden brown. Ideally served hot.

Fiori di zucchine fritti
Courgette flowers fried in batter

Make a batter with flour and water and a pinch of salt and immerse the flowers in it until fully coated. Heat some olive oil (or sunflower oil) in a deep frying pan and, when very hot, put in the flowers a few at a time. As soon as they are golden brown (a few moments) whisk them out and eat immediately.

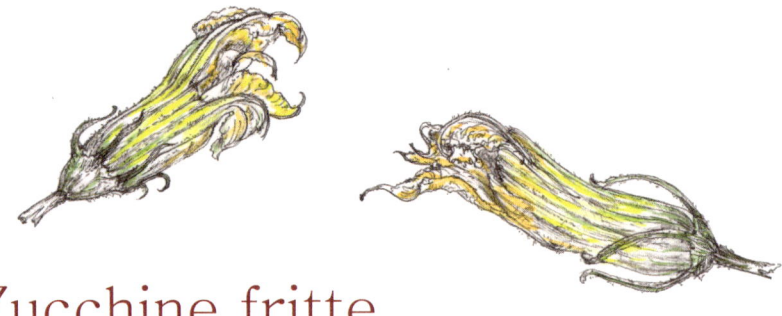

Zucchine fritte
Fried courgette slices

My uncle Peppino used to make these for his eight children – and I was often the ninth! His wife, known as 'la contina', refused to cook for supper as she had had enough by then, so he had to do it. It was a very happy arrangement: 50 years later feminists would have been proud of her.

> 3 courgettes, thinly sliced
> 1 egg beaten with a little water and a pinch of salt
> 2 tbsp flour

Salt the courgette slices and leave them to drain for an hour. Then pat dry and shake each slice in a clean cloth with flour, turn them in the egg and fry quickly until golden brown. Drain on paper, sprinkle with salt and eat immediately.

Cozze arraganate
Grilled mussels

   500g fresh mussels
   2 cloves of garlic, crushed
   5 tbsp fine homemade breadcrumbs
   3 tbsp parsley finely chopped
   4 tbsp grated parmesan
   4 tbsp extra virgin olive oil
   1 egg, beaten
   salt and pepper

Put the crumbs in a bowl and add the egg, parmesan, chopped garlic, parsley, salt and pepper. Wash and scrub the mussels, put them in a wide pan over a high heat and wait till they open (it should take no more than 3 or 4 minutes). Discard any unopened ones. Remove half of each shell and leave the mussels on the remaining half. Reserve the cooking juices.
Place the shells containing the mussels onto an oiled oven dish, making sure that you free each mollusc from its shell with a sharp knife. Moisten the breadcrumb mixture with a little of the filtered juices, making sure that the mixture does not become soggy.
Top each shell with the breadcrumb mixture, drizzle with olive oil and put under the grill for a few minutes or until the surface is golden. *My friends always long for more!*

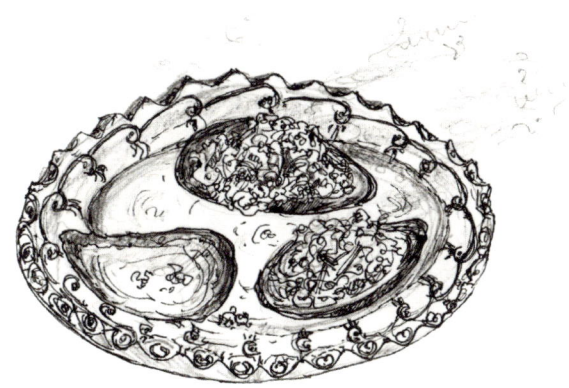

I Sott'aceti
Preserved vegetables

Pugliese women busy themselves preserving the profusion of summer vegetables for the winter months.

Aubergines, tomatoes, peppers, lambascioni and courgettes are first dried in the sun or blanched in vinegar and then steeped in olive oil, garlic and oregano.

These sott'aceti form an essential part of any antipasto misto.

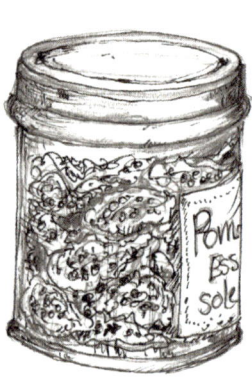
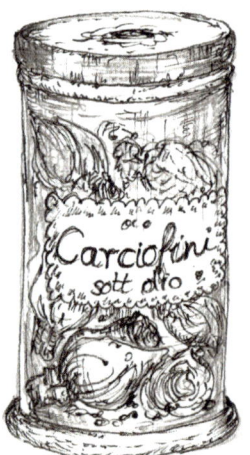
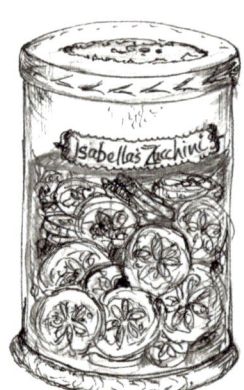

The Seasons of Puglia

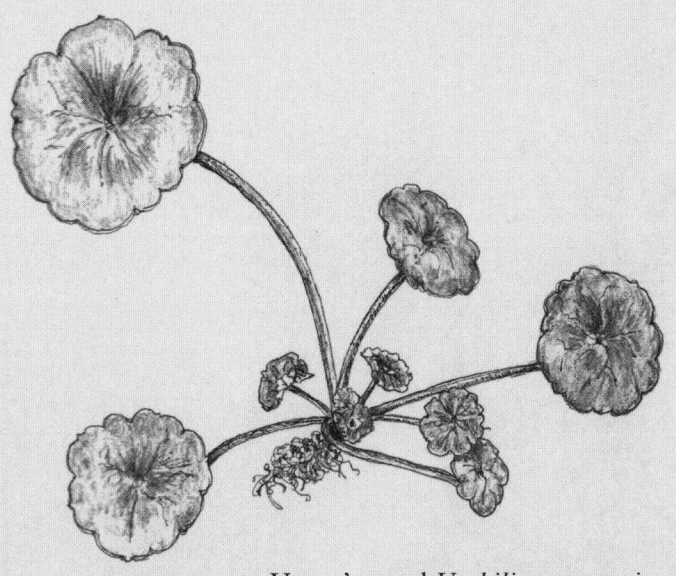

Venus's navel *Umbilicus rupestri*

Primavera

Awakening the Senses

'It is spring again. The earth is like a child that knows poems by heart.' – Rainer Maria Rilke

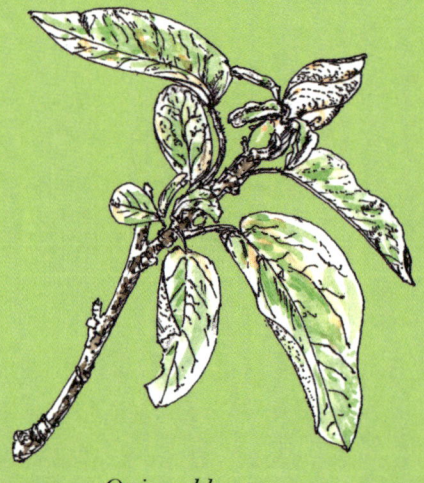

Quince blossom

Almond blossom, carpets of wild flowers, glorious blue sky and a sparkling turquoise sea: an explosion of colours means spring has arrived, though the crowds are not yet here. For us too, spring brings a desire for newness and an innate feeling of anticipation. We shed layers of clothing, and there is warmth, light, the scent of flowers and love in the air.

Erbe spontanee
Edible weeds

Gathering edible weeds is a passion shared by all of us who come from Puglia. The end of March is the time for this exciting activity: young dandelions, *lambascioni* (tassel hyacinth), nettles, young asparagus, chicory, *acetosella* (field or wood sorrel), wild fennel. Here are some ways of cooking these delicacies.

Cicorielle
Dandelions

I remember my mother sending me out to pick dandelion leaves until my hands were sticky and blackened with sap.

This is how she cooked them: clean the leaves thoroughly and cook in boiling salted water for 20 minutes. Strain and throw into a pan containing a little hot olive oil, two peeled cloves of garlic and one hot chilli pepper. Add a couple of fresh tomatoes. Toss the leaves in the juices for a couple of minutes and eat with a chunk of bread.

My English mother-in-law used to get quite anxious about me eating these while I was expecting my first child. However, I ate plenty and my children have survived the feasts!

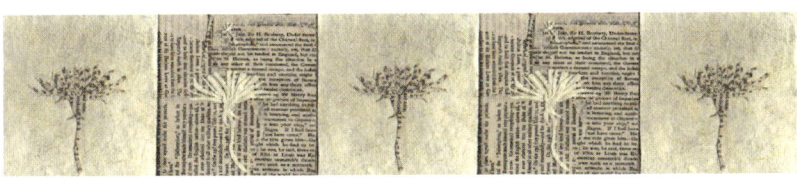

LAMBASCIONI

Tassle hyacinth

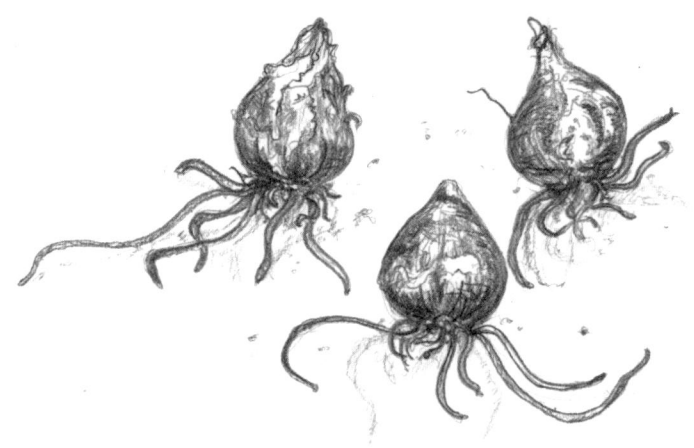

I am sure poverty forced the discovery of these edible bulbs – the rich Tuscans don't eat them, but they are delicious! They grow wild on limestone and proliferate in spring. They are dug out of the earth when three straggly leaves first appear.

The simplest way to cook *lambascioni*:
Wash the bulbs then boil them. When tender, after about 20 minutes, drain and remove the rough outer skins while still warm. Make a small incision on each one, sprinkle with salt and pour over a little olive oil and vinegar. Serve cold.

A glass of Greco di Tufo makes a perfect accompaniment.

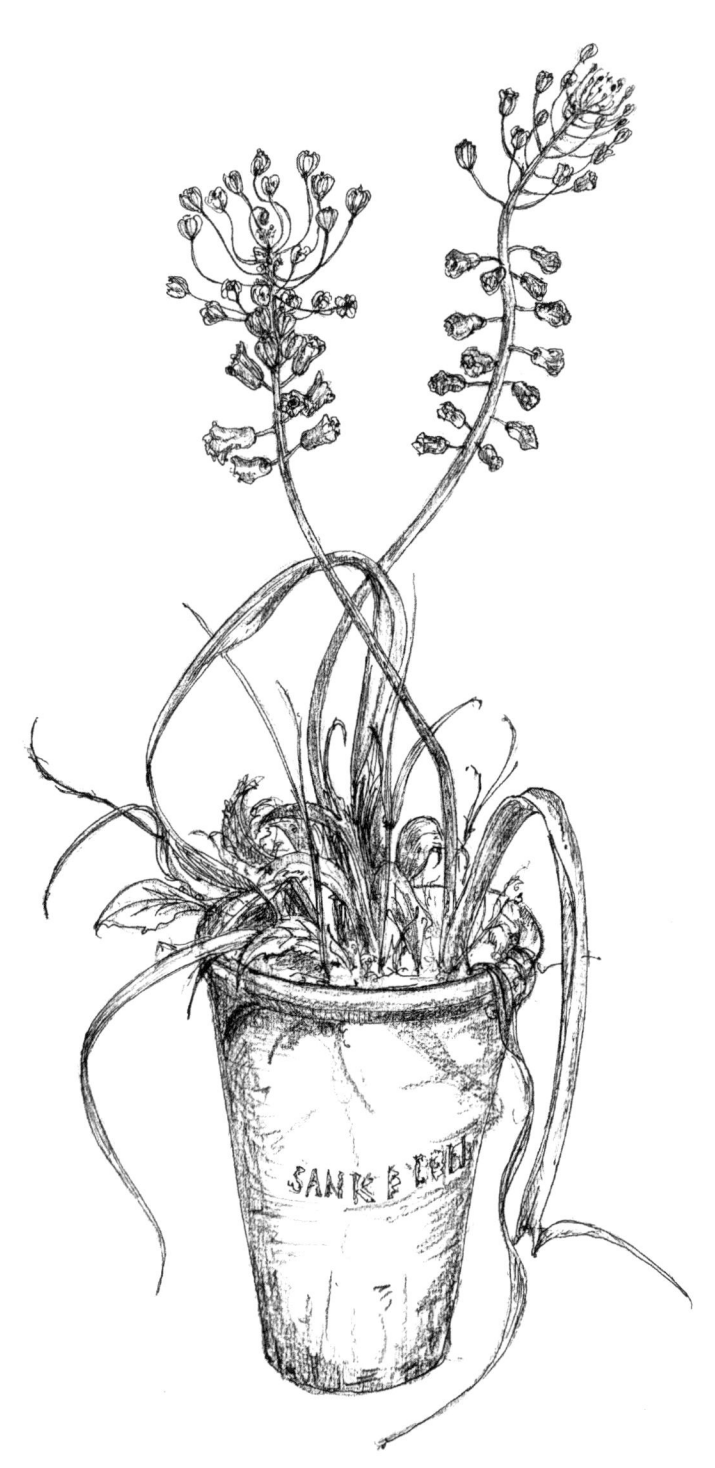

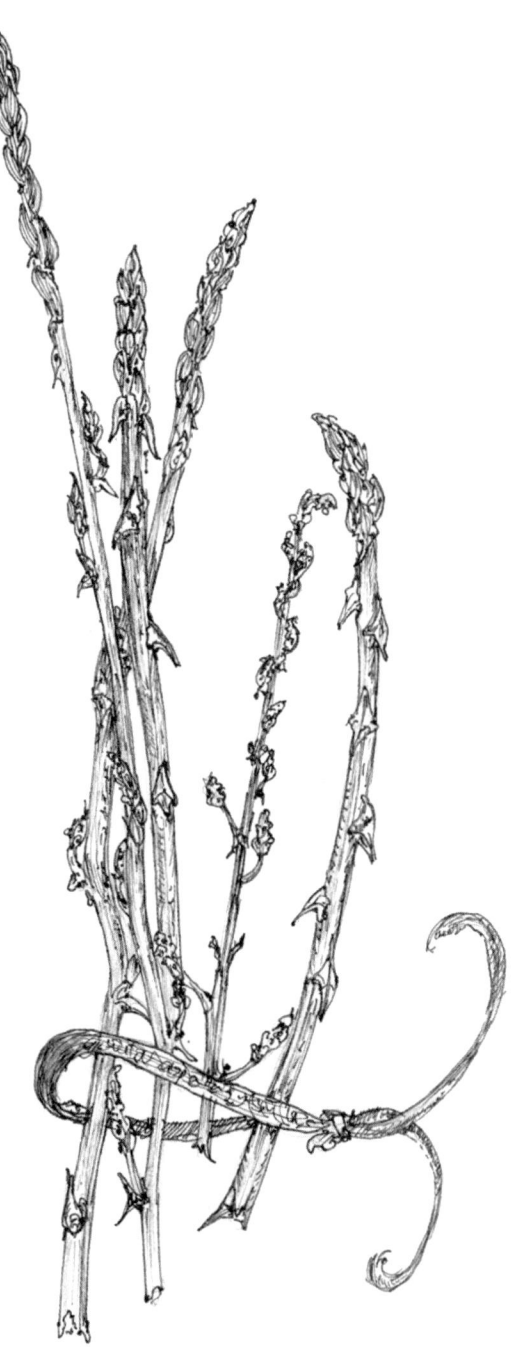

Asparago selvatico
Wild asparagus

March is the time to gather the shoots of this prickly climbing plant which grows everywhere in Puglia. When I am at the trullo I love looking for these wild asparagus in the morning and making a quick omelette for breakfast.

Fry a handful of asparagus in oil for a few moments, add three beaten eggs, season, stir the contents of the pan, fold over and serve.

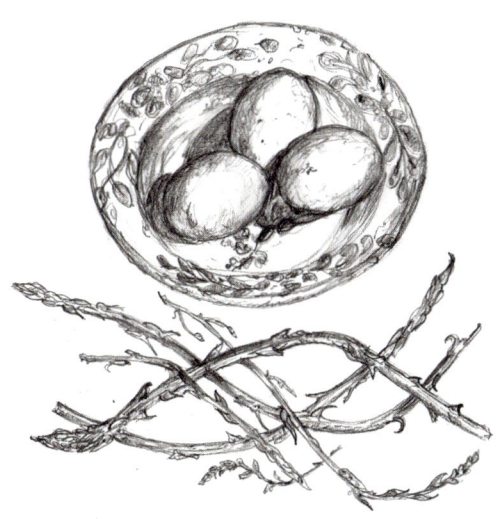

Asparago selvatico con uova

Alternatively, boil the asparagus in salted water for 5 minutes, drain and serve with olive oil, some lemon juice and salt. A delicacy.

Pasta primavera con fagiolini e pomodoro
Springtime pasta with fresh green beans and tomatoes

This wonderful recipe combines the freshest vegetables found on the market stall – bought just hours after being harvested!

> 400g fresh French beans, washed
> 400g fresh pasta (shells or spaghetti)
> 300g cherry tomatoes (or 1 tin tomatoes)
> 100g passata
> 1 red onion, sliced
> 2 tbsp extra virgin olive oil
> 2 tbsp grated *cacio ricotta* (salted ewe cheese or pecorino)
> salt, pepper

In a large pan gently fry the onion. In a separate deep pan, cook the beans for 5 mins in salted boiling water. Drain and add them to the fried onions. Add the tomatoes and passata, season and cook on a gentle heat for a further 15 minutes. In the meantime, cook the pasta in salted boiling water and, when ready, drain and pour into the bean mixture. Stir well with plenty of cheese and freshly ground pepper.

Peperoni friggitelli fritti
Fried green peppers

These are small sweet peppers that are grown in abundance from spring to summer.

>   200g peppers
>   20 small tomatoes, chopped
>   1 clove of garlic, chopped
>   3 tbsp extra virgin olive oil
>   1 small chilli (optional)
>   2 or 3 basil leaves
>   salt, pepper

Wash the *friggitelli*, pat them dry and fry them in a large frying pan until soft (about 5 mins). Add garlic, salt, chopped tomatoes and the optional chilli, and cook over a medium heat for 8-10 mins. Add basil and adjust seasoning and serve immediately. Lovely with crusty bread to mop up the juices.

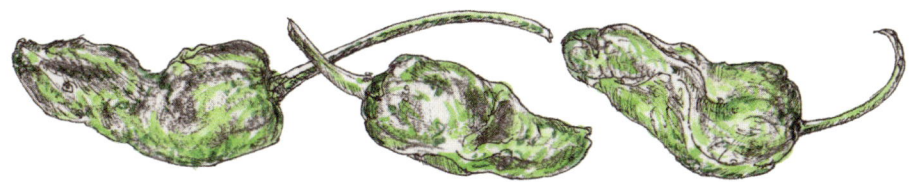

Pasta con fave e piselli
Pasta with fresh broad beans and peas

A delicious and nourishing dish, rich in minerals and vitamins.

>300g pasta (fusilli or other)
>300g fresh broad beans
>300g peas
>1 onion, finely sliced
>1 tbsp extra virgin olive oil
>1 stick celery, finely chopped.
>salt, pepper and parmesan, grated

Pod the beans and peas. In a saucepan, gently fry the onion for a couple of minutes. Add the peas, beans and celery, stir for a few more minutes. Now add 200ml warm water, season and leave to braise for 15 minutes. In a separate pan, boil the pasta and, when ready, drain and add to the peas and beans, mix well and add pepper if necessary. Sprinkle some grated parmesan on top and serve immediately.

A glass of Fiano is the ultimate pleasure with this dish.

In early spring it is a delight to eat *le fave fresche* (fresh raw broad beans) at the end of a meal. This is how we do it: prepare a little bowl with fine sea salt, now dip each fava into it and savour the fresh crunchy taste of this unique vegetable.

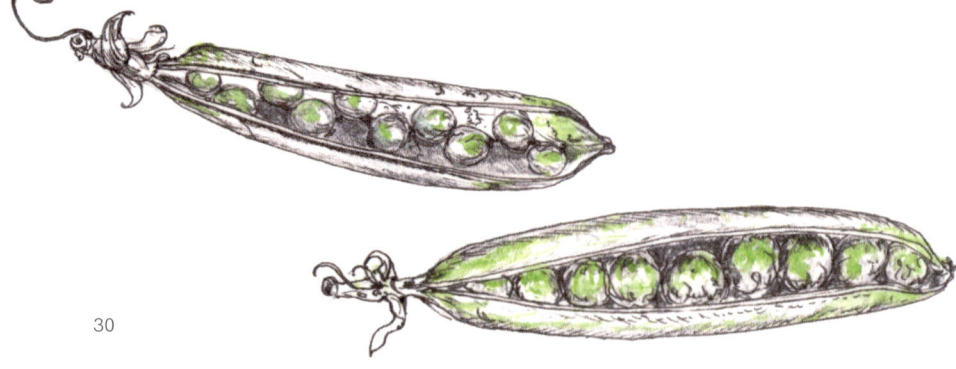

CARCIOFI

Artichokes

I can never have enough of these; when I am in Puglia, I buy a bunch of 20 for next to nothing and eat them raw (sliced and served with shavings of parmesan, a drizzle of olive oil and plenty of black pepper). They are also amazing in a risotto or a frittata, or just cut into quarters and fried in olive oil. The Pugliese variety have spikes on their stems and the leaves of each slender green bud finish in sharp points; very different from the globe variety much enjoyed by the Romans. Unfortunately, one cannot find Pugliese artichokes in the UK – not yet. But even with a substitute, the end result is still delicious.

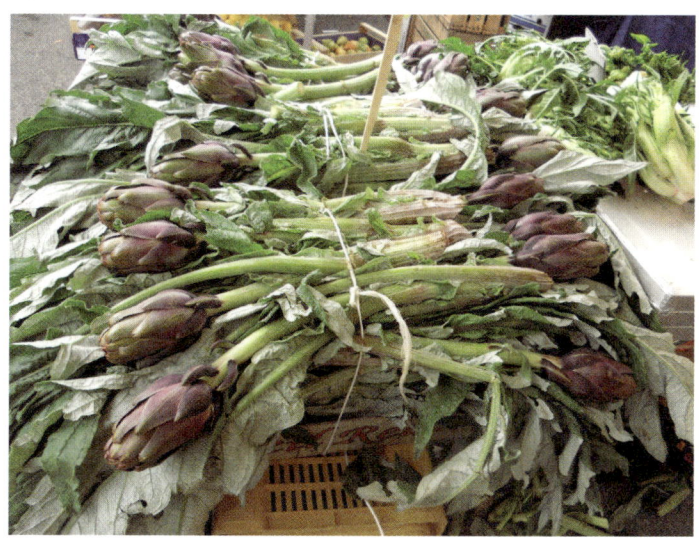

Carciofi fritti
Fried artichokes

A very simple way of preparing *carciofi*. It can be served as a side dish with fish or meat or, even better, as a *spuntino* or snack, with a drink.

>   4 small fresh artichokes
>   a plate of seasoned flour
>   2 beaten eggs with a pinch of salt
>   3 tbsp olive oil for frying

Peel back and remove the tough outer leaves and cut off the stalks at the base. Trim the spiky tops. With a very sharp knife, cut the artichokes lengthways into thin slices. Dip each slice into the flour, then into the beaten egg and fry in the bubbling hot oil until they are golden brown. As the slices are very thin, they will not take long. Drain on kitchen paper and serve immediately after sprinkling with some more salt if necessary. Addictive.

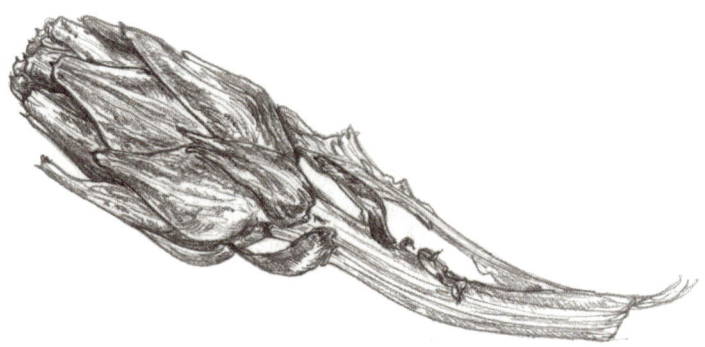

Enjoy with a good glass of Fiano.

Carciofi ripieni col sugo e pasta
Stuffed artichokes in tomato sauce served with pasta

6 artichokes: tough outer leaves removed and stalks cut off at the base so that they can stand upright in the pan.
1 large tin peeled tomatoes
1 carton tomato passata
1 clove of garlic
1 onion, chopped
400g penne or maccheroni
salt, pepper

For the stuffing mixture:
1 egg, beaten
2 cloves of garlic, chopped
1 tbsp chopped parsley
2 tbsp grated parmesan
a little bread soaked in milk
salt, pepper

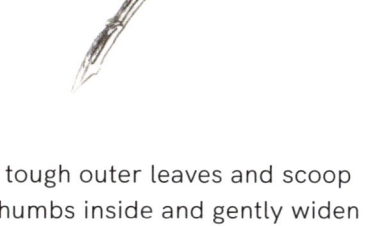

Prepare each artichoke: trim, remove tough outer leaves and scoop out the centre with a knife. Put your thumbs inside and gently widen the cavity. Mix the stuffing ingredients together and stuff the cavities.

In a deep pan, prepare a tomato sauce. Fry the thinly sliced onion in olive oil until golden and add a large tin of peeled tomatoes, the passata, garlic, salt and pepper. Now stand the artichokes in the sauce (which must almost cover them) and let the mixture bubble gently for 30 to 40 minutes.

Serve the sauce with pasta for a first course with grated parmesan, and the stuffed artichoke as a second course.

A typical Sunday lunch:
Agnello con patate
Baked lamb chops, potatoes, tomatoes and garlic

    8 lamb chops
    500g potatoes, sliced lengthwise (chip thickness)
    3 cloves of garlic, chopped
    4 to 5 tbsp extra virgin olive oil
    50g grated parmesan
    6 to 8 peeled tinned tomatoes, roughly chopped
    100ml water and 60ml wine
    chopped parsley, salt, pepper

In a deep ovenproof dish, lay the meat and potatoes quite tightly together. Sprinkle on top the garlic, chopped tomatoes, parsley, parmesan, salt and pepper. Pour the oil all over. Carefully pour around the edges of the dish half a small glass of water and a little white wine.
Cook (190°C/gas mark 5) for an hour, till golden and crispy.

A good Primitivo di Manduria is a must!

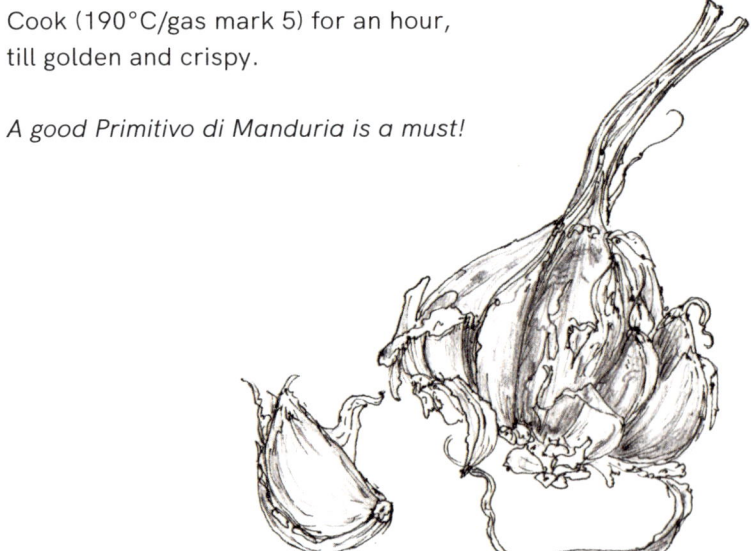

Easter Sunday lunch

Easter would not be the same without this dish. The succulent lamb and the rich aromas of fresh rosemary and garlic bring back so many happy memories. A huge family gathering – us children hugging our big Easter eggs, and women in a flurry – is inseparable from Pugliese hospitality. Everybody around the table waiting eagerly for the *festa* to begin...

Agnello al verdetto
Easter Lamb

My mother's version: For 6 people

> 1kg stewing lamb
> 50g each pecorino and parmesan cheese
> 2 eggs
> 400g fresh peas
> 1 onion, finely chopped
> plenty of parsley, finely chopped
> 1 glass dry white wine
> 3 tbsp olive oil
> a sprig of rosemary, 2 cloves of garlic, chopped, salt, pepper

Pre-heat the oven to 200°C/gas mark 6. In a large oven dish, fry the onion and garlic with olive oil. When golden, add the meat and brown it on all sides. Now add the wine, rosemary, garlic, salt and pepper. Cover and bake for 40 minutes, then remove from the oven and add the peas. Replace the lid and return to oven. Cook for a further 40 minutes then remove from oven. Beat the eggs in a bowl, add the chopped parsley, grated pecorino and parmesan cheese. Add the mixture to the dish without stirring and return to the oven for a final 5 minutes. *Negroamaro is the perfect accompaniment.*

Scarcella or 'Scarcedda'
A typical Easter cake

I used to be fascinated watching my mother make these cakes every Easter. It marks the end of Lent and is a symbol of good luck and prosperity.

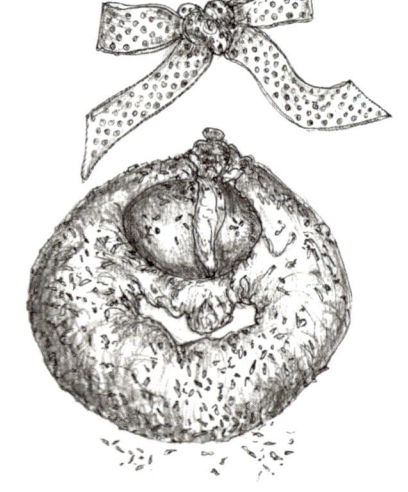

500g flour
100g sugar
½ sachet baking powder
zest of 1 lemon
100ml extra virgin olive oil
200ml milk
2 eggs
a pinch of salt
coloured sugar sprinkles

Place the flour in a bowl, make a well and add the sugar, baking powder, salt and lemon zest.
Pour in the olive oil very slowly, mixing it with a fork. Slowly add the warm milk until you have a smooth dough. Roll it to ½ inch thickness.
Divide the dough into three parts, make them into three strips, and shape them to make a basket. Place a raw egg (in its shell) in the middle of the basket.
Put the scarcella on a baking tray and brush with beaten egg and water. Add some coloured sprinkles and cook in the oven at 180°C/gas mark 4 for 30 minutes.

Estate
Fun and Games

'Dance until you shatter yourself.' – Rumi

Summer is a time of plenty. All the hard work in the fields has come to fruition. Market stalls are stacked with mountains of peaches, apricots, thirst quenching watermelons, shiny purple aubergines, glistening zucchine, fleshy red, yellow and green peppers, tasty cucumbers and the unique and treasured tomato, *poma amoris (*love apple). Since the 1500s, we Pugliese have been eating this fruit with oil, salt and pepper, as we still do.

I have early memories of lazy lunches sitting under the shade of an olive tree demolishing some simple, delightful dishes. My mother would command everyone to be seated and to start eating as soon as these piping hot dishes were brought to the table.

And always wonderful fresh fruit at the end of a meal.

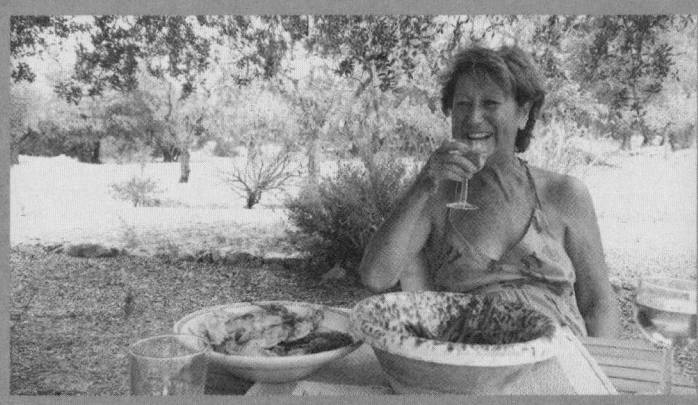

Orecchiette con pomodoro e ricotta salata

Orecchiette pasta with tomato sauce and salted ricotta

Pugliese women used to make fresh orecchiette ('little ears') most days. Now you can buy this pasta fresh or dried in shops or supermarkets. I remember Keith Floyd loving this dish when he tasted it during the filming of his BBC series *Floyd on Italy* for which I was the researcher. He defined it as 'Puglia on a plate'.

400g orecchiette pasta
500g tomatoes, deseeded
250g salted ricotta or pecorino
1 small onion, sliced
1 clove of garlic, crushed
2 tbsp extra virgin olive oil
a few basil leaves

Make a tomato sauce using fresh ripe tomatoes. Start by frying the onion and garlic gently in the olive oil. Add the deseeded tomatoes, a few basil leaves and simmer for 30 minutes. Meanwhile, cook the pasta. Drain and serve at once, topped with the sauce and a generous amount of grated ricotta or pecorino.

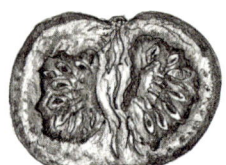 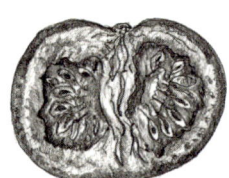 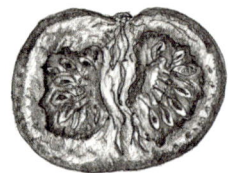

Spaghetti con pomodori al forno
Spaghetti with tomato baked in the oven

A very simple and delightful summer recipe.

    400g spaghetti
    500g ripe plum tomatoes, cut lengthways
    2 cloves of garlic, chopped
    2 tbsp grated parmesan
    a generous sprig of oregano
    3 tbsp extra virgin olive oil
    salt, pepper

Put the tomatoes into a shallow oven dish. Cover with all the ingredients and cook in a pre-heated oven at 180°C/gas mark 4 for about 30 minutes or until the tomatoes are slightly charred. Meanwhile, cook the spaghetti in plenty of salted water until al dente, drain and amalgamate with the tomatoes straight out of the oven and serve *immediately!*

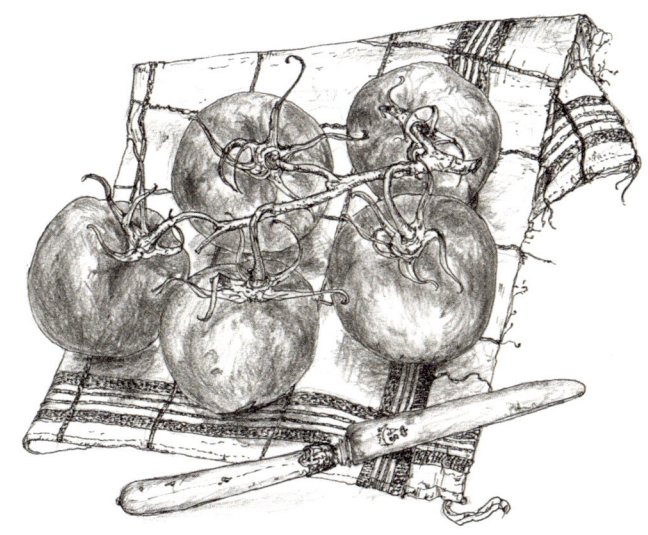

Pomodori ripieni
Stuffed tomatoes with rice

    4 beef tomatoes
    4 tbsp Arborio or Carnaroli rice
    3 potatoes (optional)
    4 tbsp olive oil
    1 big clove of garlic, crushed
    1 tbsp chopped parsley
    1 tbsp grated parmesan
    a few basil leaves
    salt, pepper

Cut across the top of tomatoes and save the lids.
With a teaspoon, take out the juice and pulp. Chop it up with a fork and put it in a large bowl. Add the rice and all the other ingredients. (The amount of oil and tomato juices should provide enough liquid for the rice to cook properly.)
Fill each tomato with the mixture, cover with a basil leaf and its lid and drizzle a little olive oil on top. Sprinkle with salt.
Put in a shallow tray, adding just enough water to cover the base so that the tomatoes do not stick at the bottom. Finally, if you fancy it, add the potatoes (cut into chips and sprinkled with salt and a little olive oil) around the edge.
Place in a hot oven and cook at around 190°C/gas mark 5 for about 40 to 45 minutes or until the potatoes are golden.
During cooking, check whether the water evaporates, in which case add a little more.

A glass of Fiano goes splendidly with this.

Zucchine alla 'poveredda'
Courgettes 'pauper style'

My mother used to cook this dish all the time and we would eat it with a chunk of bread, dipped into the delicious juice.

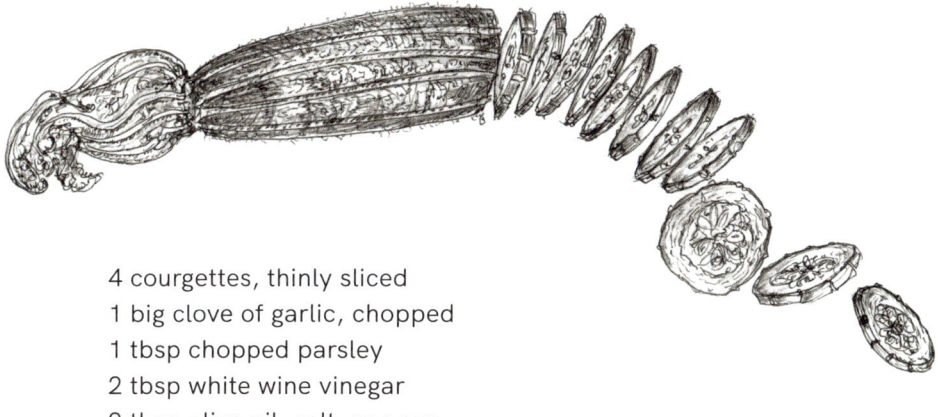

4 courgettes, thinly sliced
1 big clove of garlic, chopped
1 tbsp chopped parsley
2 tbsp white wine vinegar
2 tbsp olive oil, salt, pepper

In a frying pan, heat the olive oil and garlic.
When sizzling hot add the sliced courgettes. Season and let them fry quite fiercely for 4 to 5 minutes.
Add the vinegar and let it evaporate for a minute or so, then reduce the heat and cook the courgettes for a further 4 to 5 minutes or until soft. At the end, add the chopped parsley and serve.
It is good hot or cold.

Minestra di zucchine
Courgette soup

1kg courgettes, cut into chunks
1 onion, finely chopped
2 tbsp parsley, chopped
2 eggs
grated parmesan
salt, pepper

Fry the sliced onion till golden. Add the courgettes, parsley, salt and pepper. Barely cover with water and cook until soft. In the meantime, in a separate bowl beat two eggs and add the grated parmesan. Add the egg mixture to the cooked courgettes and, as soon as the eggs begin to harden, remove from the pan and serve the soup with bread croutons.

'O mangi questa minestra o salti dalla finestra'
'beggars can't be choosers'

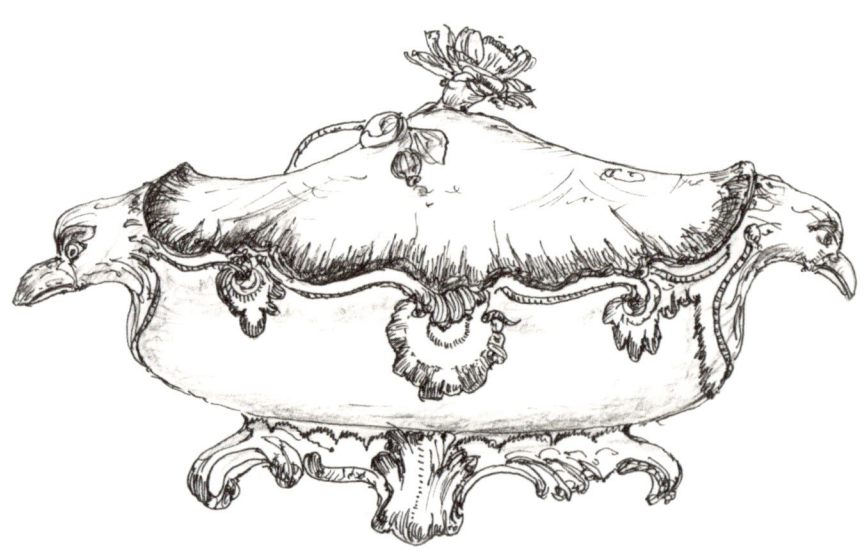

Parmigiana di melanzane
Aubergines with mozzarella and parmesan

3 large aubergines, sliced and salted
500g ripe tomatoes, peeled and chopped
2 cloves of garlic, peeled and left whole
1 onion, finely chopped
bunch of basil, chopped (by hand!)
1 large mozzarella, sliced
4 tbsp parmesan cheese, grated
1 tsp sugar
a little flour
2 eggs, beaten with a little water
3 tbsp extra virgin olive oil
6 to 7 tbsp sunflower oil
salt, pepper

Slice the aubergines lengthwise, salt and leave for half an hour to let the juices run out.
Make a tomato sauce. Fry the onion and garlic in the olive oil until soft and fragrant. Add the tomatoes, basil, sugar, salt and pepper and cook vigorously for 6-8 minutes, then let it simmer for 20 minutes. Remove the whole garlic cloves.
Pat dry the aubergines slices, dust them with flour, dip in beaten egg and fry in hot oil until golden brown. Turn them over once while frying. Drain them on absorbent paper. In a baking dish, layer the aubergines, sliced mozzarella, parmesan and basil with the tomato sauce. Top with freshly grated parmesan and bake in a medium hot oven until bubbling and unmistakably ready (about 30 minutes). Good hot or cold.

No argument – this is the authentic Pugliese method!

Peperoni arrosto con acciughe, capperi e aglio

Roast peppers with anchovies, capers and garlic

    3 or 4 peppers
    6 salted anchovy fillets, chopped
    2 cloves of garlic, chopped
    2 tbsp parsley, chopped
    2 tsp capers
    salt, pepper
    extra virgin olive oil

Grill the peppers until the skin is slightly charred. Remove and place in a plastic bag for 5 minutes. Remove and peel the peppers; cut them into slices and place on a serving dish.
Add all the ingredients, finishing with a generous drizzle of olive oil. Delicious served hot or cold, with crunchy bread.

Cialdedda

Cold summer soup

    2 red onions
    3 tomatoes
    1 cucumber
    1 tsp oregano
    3 tbsp olive oil

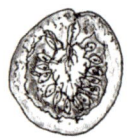 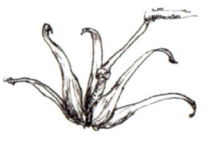 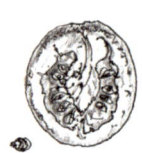

Slice the onions, tomatoes and cucumber. Add some water (just enough to moisten the raw ingredients) and an ice cube, plus the olive oil and oregano. Mix and add salt and pepper to taste. Serve in soup bowls with slices of good bread.

Ideal for those torrid Pugliese summer days....

Italians NEVER eat salad with pasta!

MANDORLE

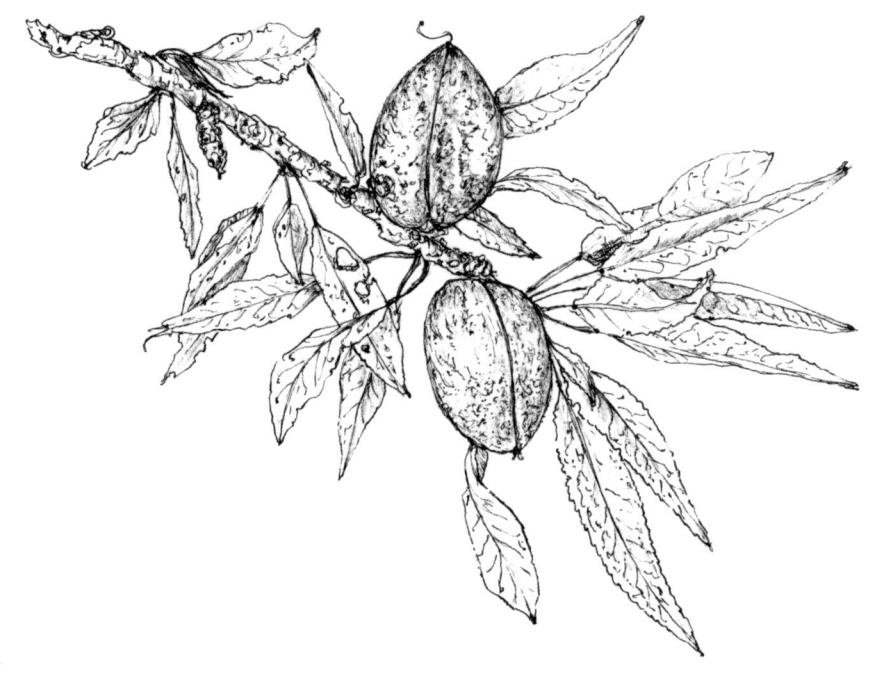

Almonds

In February and March magic falls over the Puglia landscape: beautiful fields of white and pink almond blossom give us hope that spring is around the corner. This is nature at its best.

In early Summer the almonds are soft and milky and can be added to salads or you can wait for them to ripen in August when they are harvested. The Toritto variety is the best.

Almonds have always been considered a luxurious crop that brings good fortune: the Romans cherished them. Cleopatra bathed in their milk to enhance her skin.

They are one of the most sociable of foods – nibbled with a drink (toast in the oven or in a thick frying pan then toss in salt) – or ground and made into delicious sweetmeats that are eaten to celebrate birthdays, weddings, Easter and Christmas.

They are also rich in proteins and many vitamins and thought to be beneficial against diseases like diabetes, high cholesterol, cancer, obesity and hair loss!

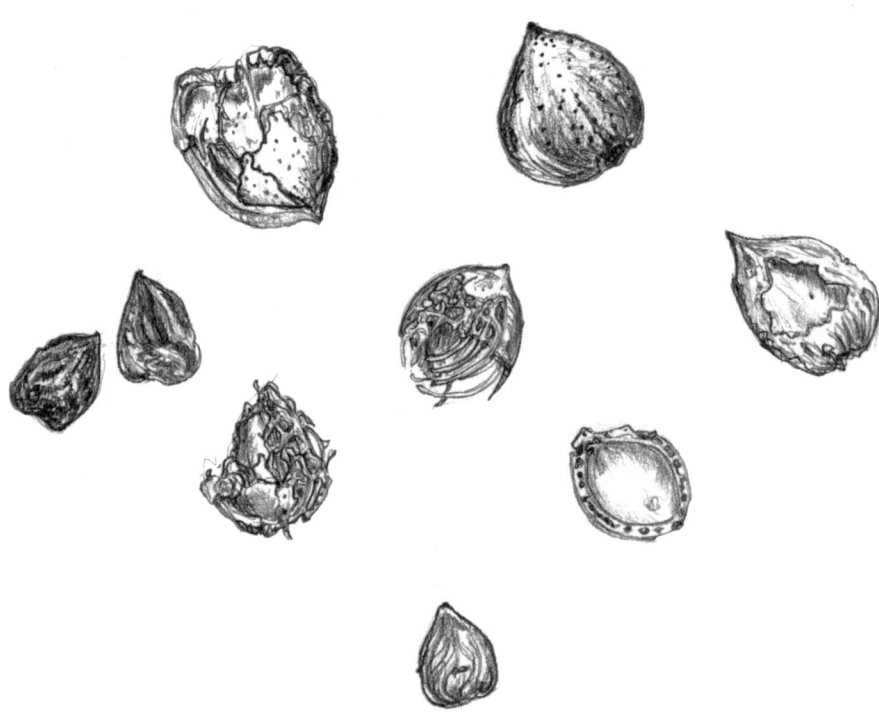

Marzapani

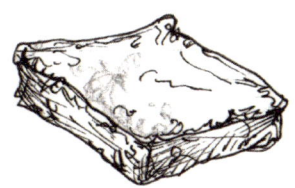

500g peeled and ground almonds
400g sugar
1 egg
1 tsp vanilla essence
1 tbsp marsala
zest and juice of ½ lemon

Mix all the ingredients on a floured wooden board and work the mixture to form a long fat sausage. Flatten this with your fingers and cut into 5 to 6cm long diamond shapes to obtain about 20 marzapani. Place on a buttered oven tray and cook in pre-heated oven at 180°C/gas mark 4 for 15 to 20 minutes.

Tarallini 'Occhi di Santa Lucia'

To eat at Christmas with toasted almonds.

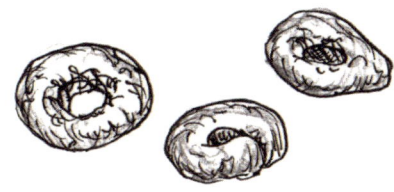

500g flour
100g olive oil
50g sugar
4 tbsp icing sugar
400g peeled and toasted almonds

Mix together the flour, olive oil and sugar into a dough. Roll out thickly and cut into 5 to 7cm long strips. Roll with your hands to make a cylinder and make into rings around your finger. Place the tarallini onto oiled greaseproof paper and bake at 180°C/gas mark 4 for about 15 minutes or until they are golden brown.
Mix the icing sugar with a little tepid water to a thick consistency. When cool, pour the tarallini and almonds into the icing sugar mixture and stir them gently so that they are well glazed all over.

Autunno

Shedding all

'As in the autumn-time the leaves fall off. First one and then another, till the branch unto the earth surrenders all its spoils.'
Dante, *Inferno*

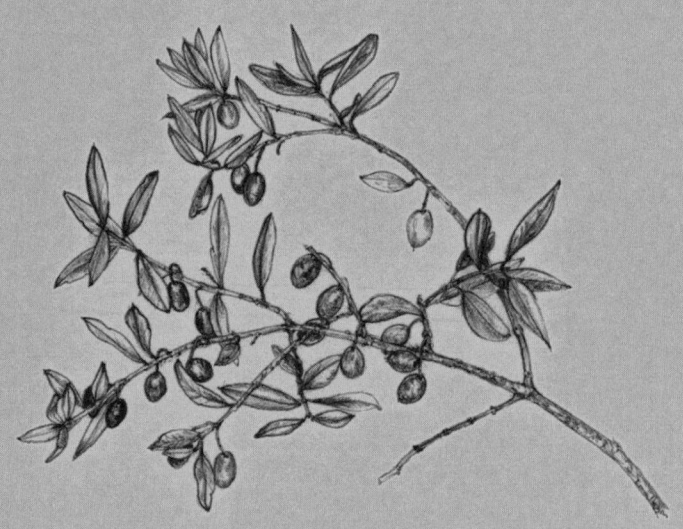

Autumn is the season when the glorious colours and rich fruitfulness are matched by the labour intensive olive picking, which happens feverishly throughout the region between late October and January. There are around 50 million olive trees in Puglia. Wherever you look you will see arms stretched up towards the branches, gathering the riches that have been nurtured for centuries.

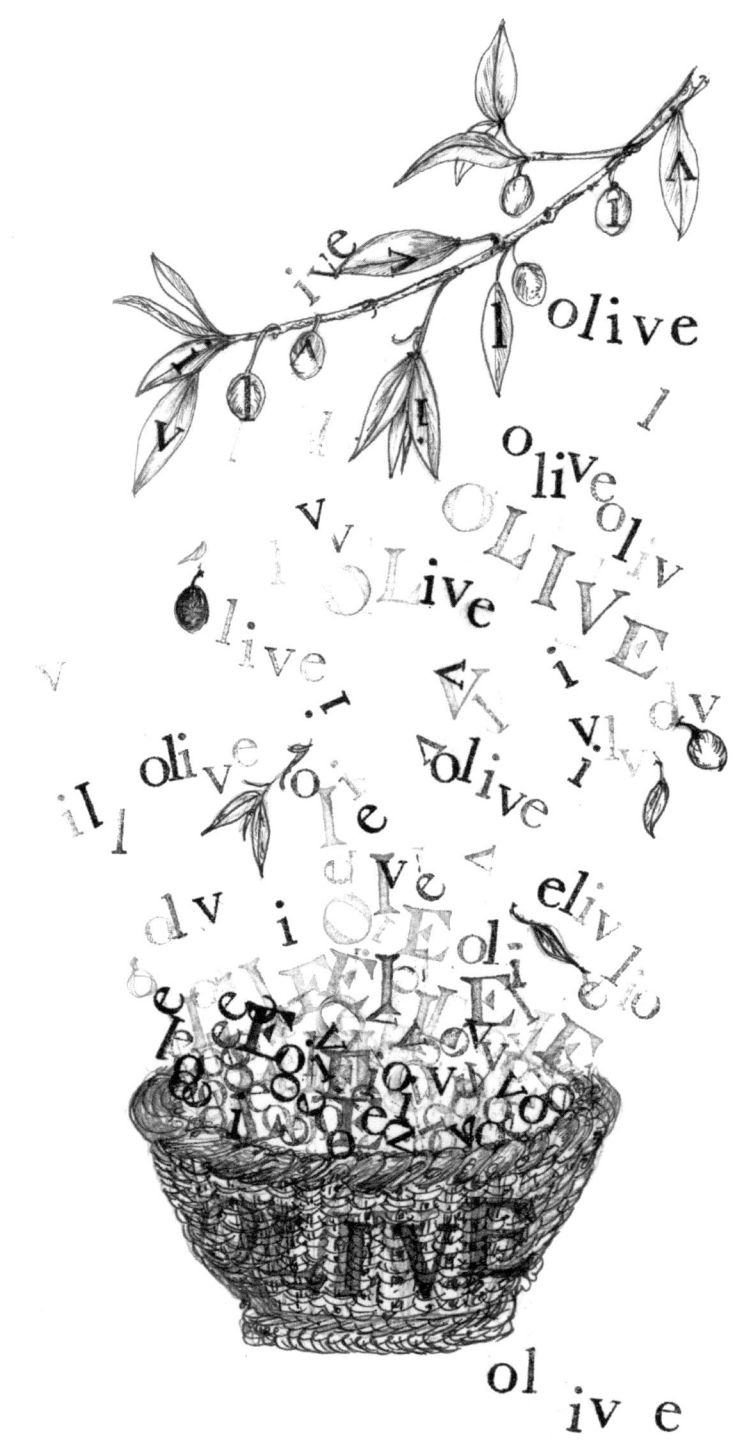

About olive oil: picking and pressing the olives

The best oil comes from olives that are hand-picked before they are completely ripe and black. My memory goes back to when I was four or five years old and the whole family (mothers, grandmothers, cousins, nephews) gathered at the olive grove. First, all of us children were settled on blankets with morsels of bread to keep us happy. Then the men would climb the trees and the women would gather the fallen olives – a back-breaking activity.

As Patience Gray eloquently writes in her book, *Honey from a Weed*: '*Like the pains of childbirth, one quickly forgets the olive-picking pains. In childbirth you are on your own, while in the olive field the ordeal is endured in good company*'. It has always been said that the most important thing is to press the freshly picked olives in a cold press; that is, to grind them between stones in the old-fashioned way and not in a machine. This is *Olio di Prima Spremitura:* pure olive oil, unaffected by heat and therefore retaining all its flavour and colour. However, with today's advanced technology, it is possible to obtain similarly excellent quality when it has been pressed in a machine. The best oil is of this year's making: keep it longer and its taste vanishes.

The rhythm of olive oil has lasted for over two-and-a-half-thousand years. Should this disappear, not only would the region's cuisine and economy suffer terribly but, most importantly, the landscape would be unrecognizable. A lot has been written about olive oil. Excited conversations go on everywhere comparing yield, acidity and colour: the darker and greener, the stronger the taste. And your own is, of course, *always the best!*

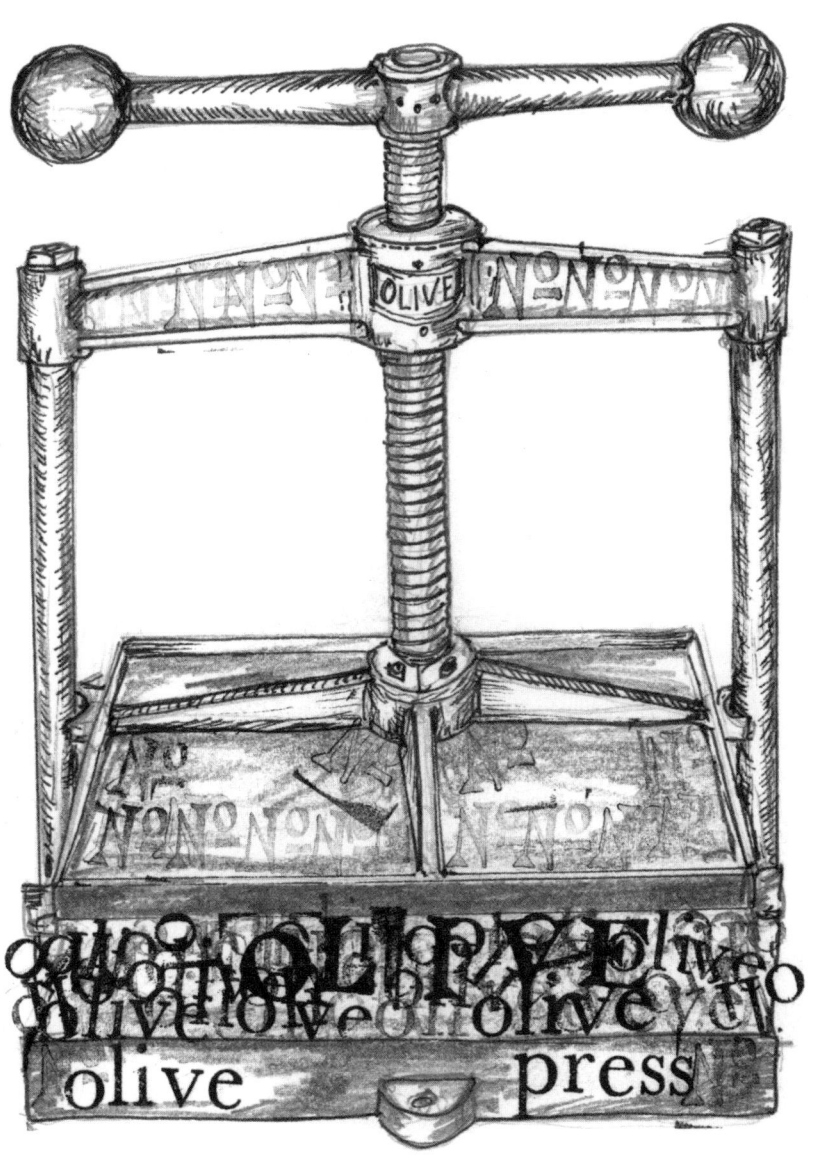

Olive fresche fritte
Fresh fried olives

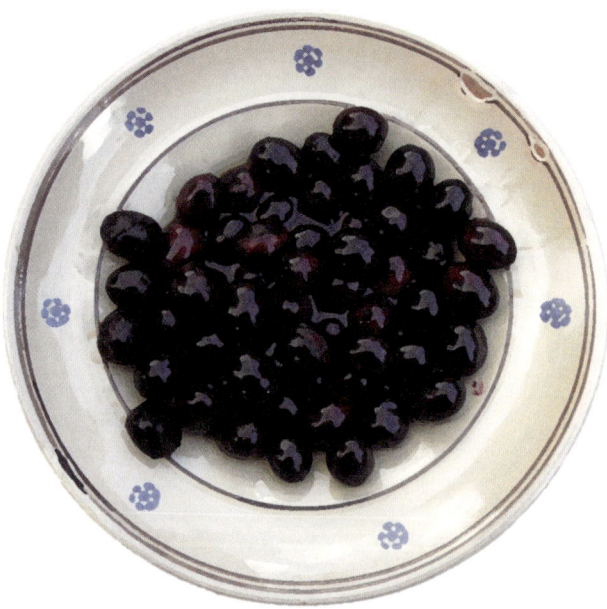

Some kinds of olive tree (mine is called *pasola*) produce olives that are suitable for frying when ripe. They don't need lengthy soaking in brine. They are simply gathered and fried in olive oil for a couple of minutes and then scattered with salt.

Eat immediately. The taste is slightly bitter, but delicious with bread and a glass of Primitivo.

Verdure d'autunno e inverno

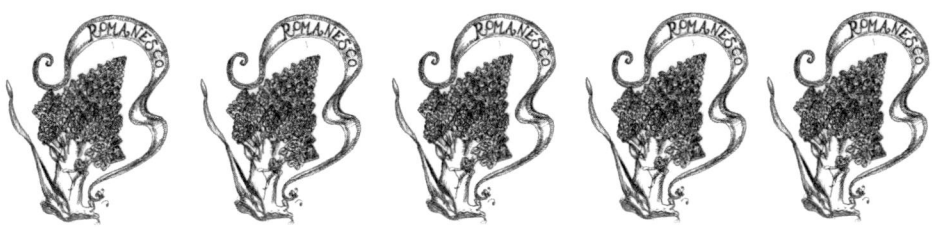

Autumn and winter vegetables

We have a passion for youth and freshness, for grasping what the season has to give at the precise moment. In smart English restaurants, they often serve a sorbet between courses to clear the palate. We like to eat chunks of raw fennel or chicory, without dressing.

Monday morning at Cisternino: stalls full of fresh local produce, nothing is imported. Tender spinach, tasty spinach beet, orange winter pumpkins, beautiful cauliflowers with spiral inflorescences, winter salads deriving from the wild *Cichorium indivia* (the tousled kind with a blanched heart), the very crisp *Scarola* and *Catalogna,* a gigantic dark leaf green chicory which looks like overgrown dandelions. And, of course, the ubiquitous *Cime di rape*, the stars of autumn. All are used or cooked in so many ways: boiled, stewed, fried, stuffed. Yet the basic ingredients are always the same: extra virgin olive oil, parsley, basil, lemon, garlic, breadcrumbs and the occasional shaving of parmesan.

Finocchi in insalata
Fennel salad

In late summer, it is wonderful to see mountains of fennel bulbs in markets everywhere. Fennel is also a delight in winter, its clean taste the ideal accompaniment for any fish or meat dish.

   2 small tender fennel bulbs
   3 tbsp extra virgin olive oil
   juice of ½ a lemon
   salt, freshly ground black pepper

Trim the bulbs, discarding any coarse outside leaves. Cut the fennel into vertical thin strips. Mix in an open dish with oil, lemon juice, salt and pepper. Leave for 10 minutes before serving.

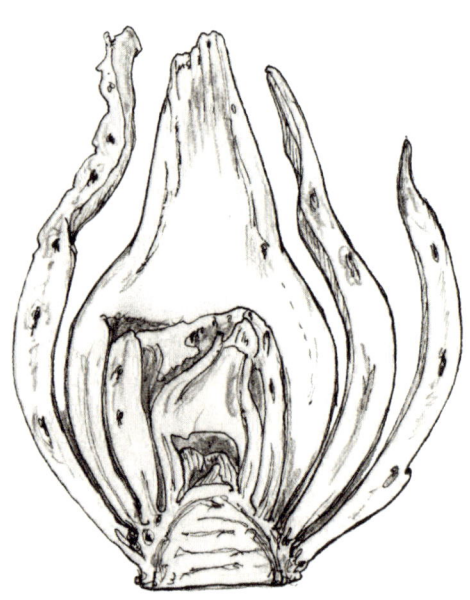

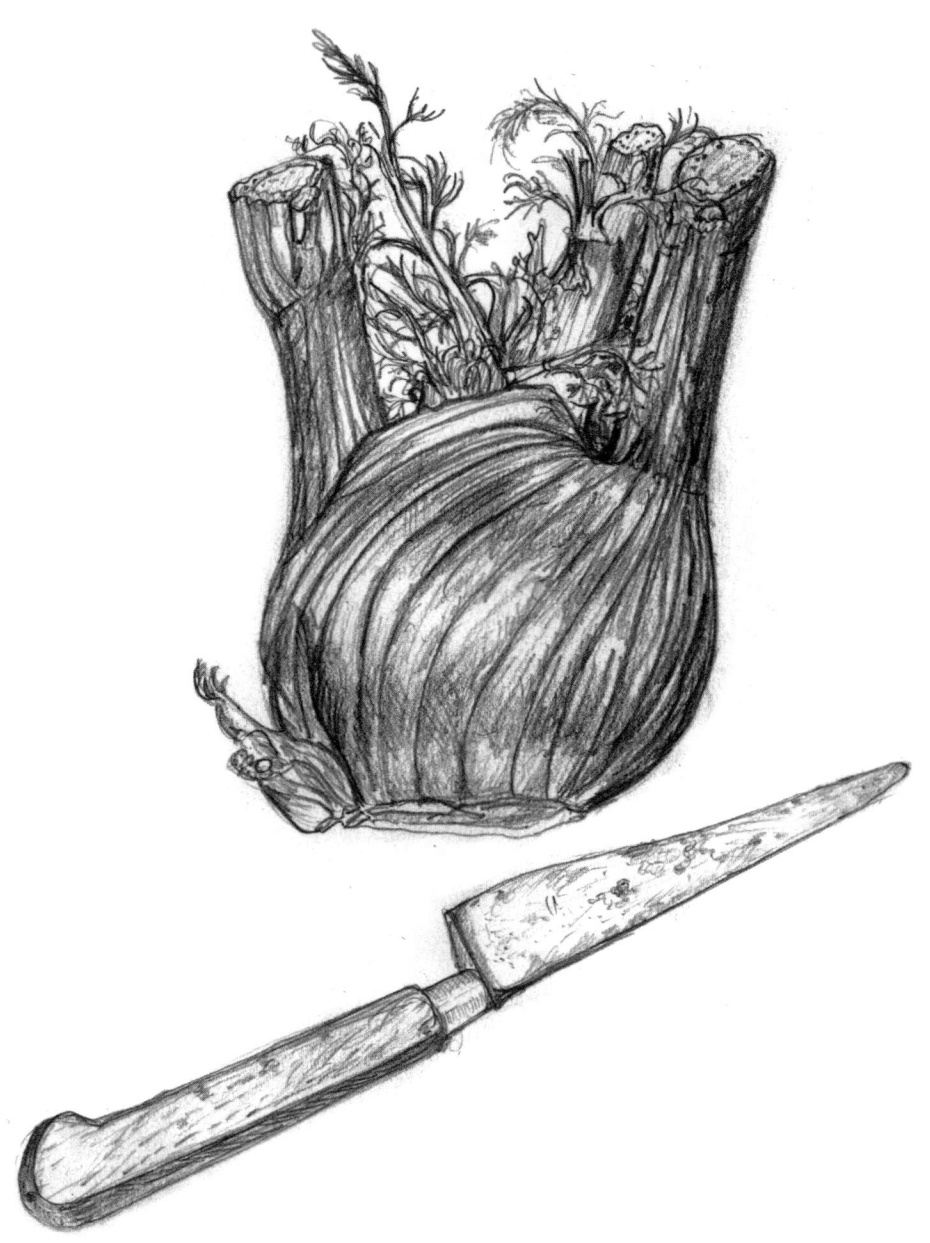

Finocchi con olio e parmigiano
Braised fennel with parmesan

I love cooking this quick dish for lunch. It is simple and satisfying.

   2 small tender fennel bulbs
   3 tbsp extra virgin olive oil
   ⅓ glass of water
   1 tbsp grated parmesan
   salt, pepper

Prepare fennel as for previous recipe. Pour the oil into a shallow pan. When hot, add the fennel slices and stir for a couple of minutes. Add the water and salt, and simmer gently until the fennel is tender – about 15 minutes. Before serving, sprinkle with the grated parmesan and freshly ground pepper.
Mop up the juices with rustic bread.

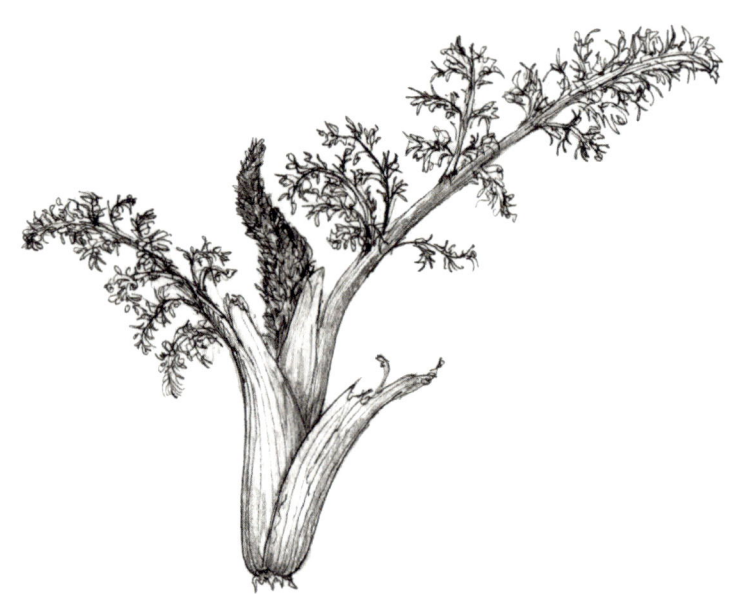

Insalata di puntarelle
Salad of young chicory shoots

Puntarelle (chicory heads) is a beautiful plant with vivid green leaves and a white centre, to be found only in Italy. The Romans loved it: they still do. The outer leaves are incredibly bitter – it is a chicory after all – and can be washed and boiled briefly before being dressed in olive oil and lemon. The inner stalk heads make this delicious salad.

> Puntarelle sliced vertically into thin strands
> 2 cloves of garlic finely chopped
> 3 tbsp extra virgin olive oil
> 2 tbsp white wine vinegar (or better, apple vinegar)
> 2 or 3 chopped anchovies (optional)
> salt, pepper

Wash the puntarelle slices and soak them in a lot of icy cold water for at least an hour. This removes some of the bitterness and makes them even crunchier. Drain and mix in a bowl with all the ingredients and serve with crunchy bread.

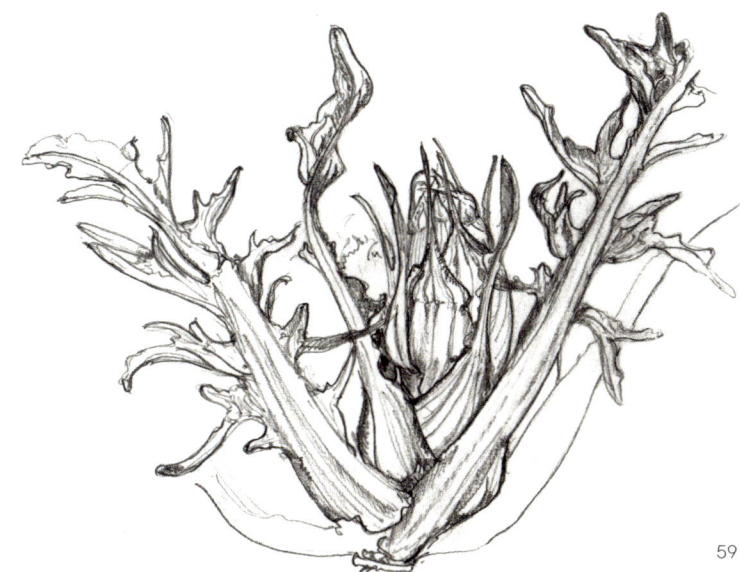

Zucca al forno con merluzzo
Baked pumpkin with cod

This dish is perfect on a winter's day. It also works very well without the cod and more topping.

> 600g cod, skinned
> 600g pumpkin, peeled and cut into slices 2 cms thick
> 5 anchovies in olive oil, chopped
> 2 tbsp of capers
> 2 cloves of garlic finely chopped
> a handful of black olives
> 4 tbsp olive oil, salt, pepper
> 3 heaped tbsp grated pecorino cheese
> 2 tbsp breadcrumbs
> some parsley

Lay half of the pumpkin slices in an oiled baking dish. Scatter half of the capers, garlic, anchovies, olives and pecorino cheese on top, sprinkle with olive oil, salt and pepper. Lay the fish on top (add a pinch of salt) and cover with the remaining slices of pumpkin topped with all the other remaining ingredients. Finish with salt and pepper, breadcrumbs and a generous drizzle of olive oil. Bake in a hot oven for about 45 minutes – the pumpkin should look crisp and golden.

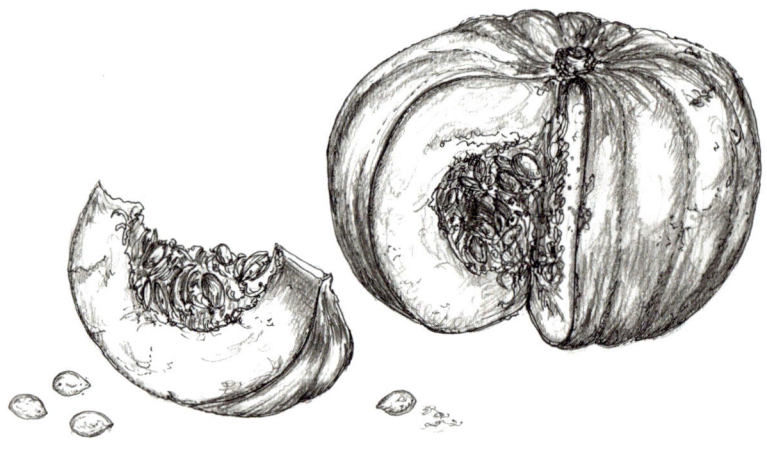

Zucca alla ricotta forte
Pumpkin with piquant ricotta salata or grated pecorino

My mother liked to make this dish on Fridays. It uses similar ingredients to the previous recipe, but the pumpkin is cut into cubes. Pumpkin needs strong flavours to enhance its delicate taste.

- 600g pumpkin, peeled and cut into small cubes
- 1 stick of celery, chopped
- 1 clove of garlic, chopped
- a small sliced onion
- 2 anchovies (tinned), chopped
- 1 tbsp of capers
- a handful of black olives
- 2 tbsp olive oil, salt, pepper
- 1 heaped tbsp grated pecorino cheese, or ricotta salata
- toasted rustic bread – *pane nostrano*

In a large pan, heat olive oil and fry the garlic, onions, capers, chopped celery and anchovies. Stir for 4 or 5 minutes, add the pumpkin and keep stirring until it turns a luscious golden colour. Add the olives, salt and a little water and cook on a low heat for about 15 minutes or until the pumpkin is soft. Add some ricotta forte or grated pecorino, then remove from the heat and serve hot with toasted bread.

Gravina Bianco, a dry, fresh and delicate white wine, would complement this dish.

Zuppa di cavolfiore
Cauliflower soup

    1 large cauliflower
    4 tbsp tomato passata
    2 cloves of garlic
    ½ red chilli
    2 tbsp extra virgin olive oil
    salt and pepper

Heat the olive oil in a deep pan. When the oil is hot, throw in the roughly chopped garlic and cook until golden before adding the washed and chopped cauliflower florets and the chilli. Stir for half a minute, add the passata, then pour over enough water to cover the cauliflower. Season and let it cook slowly until tender.

Delicious with toasted Pugliese bread drizzled with a generous amount of olive oil. You can also add some small pasta to the soup (when the cauliflower is al dente) and serve it with grated parmesan.

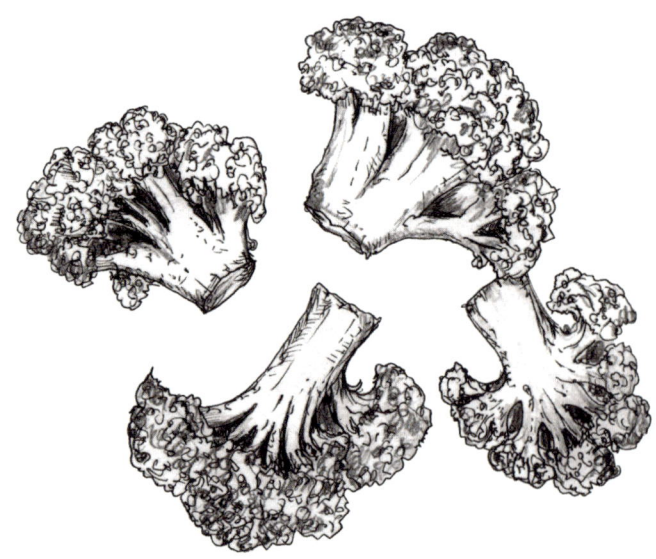

FUNGHI

Wild mushrooms

My mother taught me how to recognise edible mushrooms and they are one of my obsessions. Autumn arrives and mushroom mania grips us Italians like a fever. In late September, I can't walk into a wood without having my nose firmly to the ground and, at the sight of one of my favourite species, like the cep, (*Boletus edulis*) I will literally jump up and down with joy!

When I came to England in the late sixties, I very rarely came across other mushroom hunters – apart from the occasional encounter with a Pole or a Russian, searching with the same concentration and intensity as I was. Things have changed however. The influence of Antonio Carluccio means that more people are on the look out for wild mushrooms, and recent laws prohibiting mushroom hunting mean that I have to be somewhat constrained.

Funghi porcini trifolati
Ceps with garlic and parsley

    800g fresh porcini mushrooms (or any of your choice)
    2 cloves of garlic, finely sliced
    5 tbsp extra virgin olive oil
    2 tbsp chopped parsley
    salt, pepper

Cep mushrooms hate contact with water, so get rid of all the detritus with a sharp knife and a damp cloth. Slice finely, and add to sizzling olive oil and garlic. Cook fiercely for about 5-7 minutes and add chopped parsley, salt and pepper just before serving.

Mop up the juices with a chunk of fresh bread and enjoy, of course, a nice glass of red.

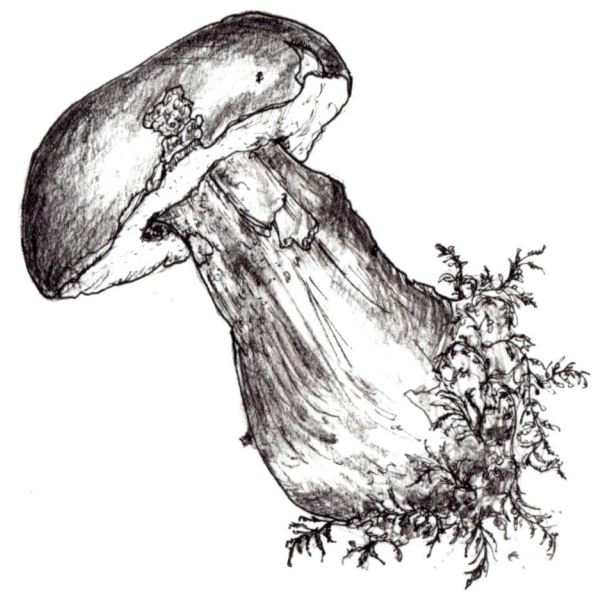

Boletus edulis
picked in Wales, 23rd September 2018

Pollo con funghi porcini
Chicken with wild mushrooms

A *pollo ruspante* (farmyard chicken) would be ideal, but almost impossible to find in cities.

- 1 chicken cut into boned pieces
- 2 rashers of bacon, chopped
- 1 tbsp butter
- 2 tbsp olive oil
- 120ml dry white wine
- 2 cloves of garlic, coarsely chopped
- 1 chopped onion
- 500g fresh porcini (or a handful of dried porcini mushrooms, soaked in tepid water for ½ hour plus 250g fresh flat capped mushrooms)
- 4 ripe tomatoes, peeled and chopped
- 3 sage leaves
- 1 bay leaf
- 2 cloves
- salt, pepper

Heat the olive oil and butter, soften the onion. Quickly fry the chicken pieces and the bacon until golden brown all over. Add the wine and let it evaporate, then add tomatoes, drained mushrooms, herbs and cloves. Season with salt and pepper and cook for about 40 minutes or until tender.

Serve with mashed potatoes, a green salad and a superb glass of Aglianico.

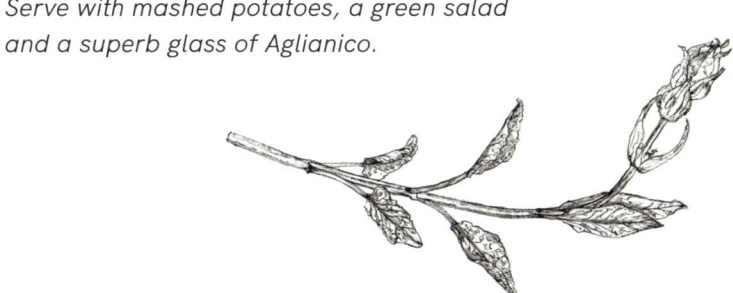

14 November 2011

Lunch
(outside)

Fresh olives – fried in olive oil

Cime di Rapa – boiled, eaten with cooking water, lemon, olive oil & pepper

Globe artichokes & eggs

with local bread + wine

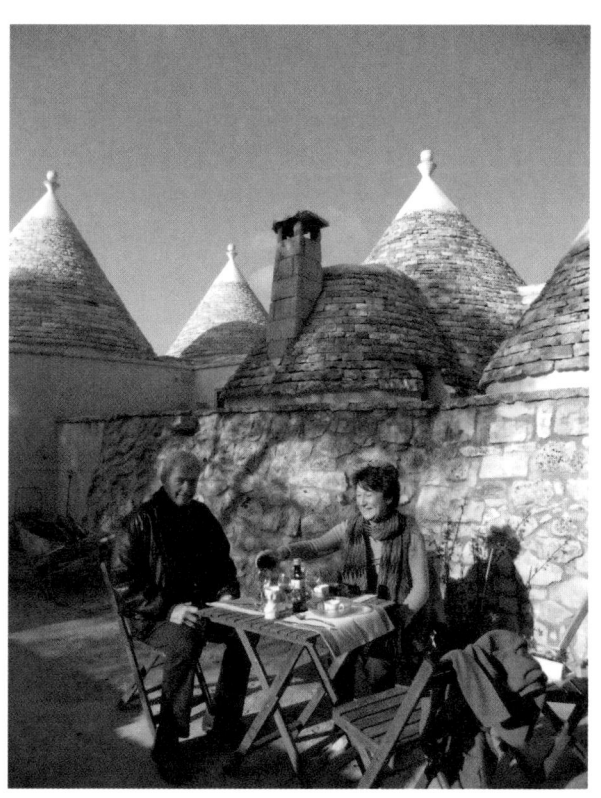

Inverno

Time for reflection

'Let us love winter, for it is the spring of genius.'
Pietro Aretino

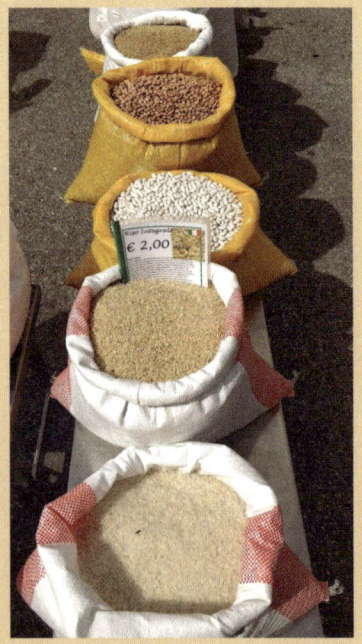

A typical market stall in Ostuni.

This is the time when all those dried and preserved foods are used in the kitchen. When I was a child, meat was scarce and usually only eaten on Sundays. On weekdays we were nourished by dishes of beans or pulses cooked in endless ways, with or without pasta, accompanied with pickled peppers or cucumber.

Orecchiette con cime di rape
Orecchiette pasta with turnip tops

This is the most typical Pugliese speciality, and it can divide people: Keith Floyd declared: 'this dish is horrible'! However, Rick Stein was full of admiration when he watched the nonna making orecchiette. She worked so swiftly and deftly, as if it was the simplest thing in the world. (I worked at different times with both Keith Floyd and Rick Stein as a researcher for their Italian television series.)

Turnip tops are sold everywhere in Puglia but they are not yet available in the UK. I have substituted broccoli in the recipe below, but you could also use cavolo nero. Curiously, the turnips themselves are never included in Pugliese cuisine.

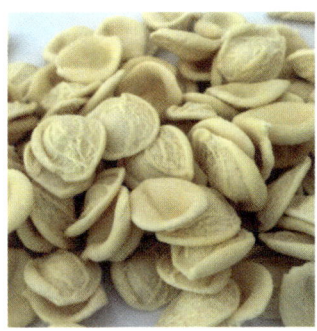

400g orecchiette
500g broccoli, trimmed into small florets (or cime di rape)
2 cloves of garlic, chopped
50g anchovies in olive oil, drained
1 fresh or dry hot red chilli
1 small bay leaf (optional)
6 tbsp extra virgin olive oil
salt, pepper

Cook the broccoli florets in plenty of salted boiling water for about 5 minutes, then add the pasta and cook until al dente. Meanwhile, in a large saucepan, heat the olive oil and sauté the garlic with the anchovies and the chilli pepper. Add the drained pasta, broccoli, and the bay leaf, mix together and sauté for a further 2 minutes. If you prefer a richer taste, add a drizzle of extra virgin olive oil and freshly ground black pepper to each plate.

Fave e cicoria
Pureed broad beans with steamed wild chicory

For centuries, this food has satisfied the hunger of many a peasant family. It is a deliciously simple dish. The green chicory, typical of Puglia, has a slightly bitter taste, and is a great accompaniment to the smooth, silky texture of the mashed beans. Little green fried peppers can be served as a side dish. A delicacy.

    350g dried broad beans, soaked overnight
    1kg wild chicory or Swiss chard
    3 small potatoes, peeled and diced
    a generous amount of extra virgin olive oil
    salt

Drain the beans and throw into a large saucepan. Add the peeled diced potato, cover with cold water, bring to the boil and simmer (stirring from time to time to avoid lumps) until it is mushy and the water has completely evaporated. Add the extra virgin olive oil, season and mash vigorously with a wooden spoon until you get a silky smooth purée. Meanwhile, steam the chicory/Swiss chard until soft, drain and serve side by side with the broad bean purée. Drizzle with extra virgin olive oil and freshly milled pepper.

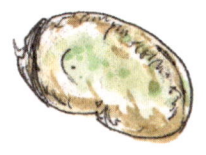 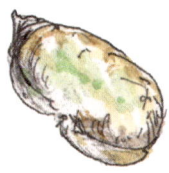 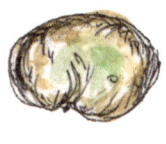 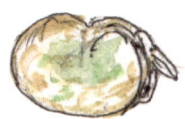

'Abstain from beans.' – Plutarch
(Plutarch must have known that people with favism, like myself, would risk their lives by eating them!)

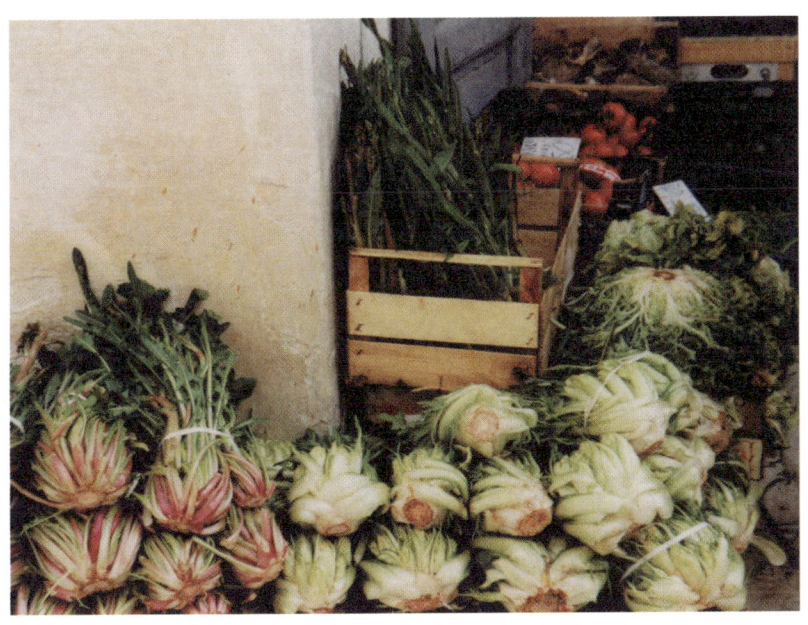

*Vegetable shop in Martina Franca, Puglia,
selling a variety of green chicories.*

Pasta e patate
Pasta and potato soup

This filling soup used to be a staple dish in winter, very welcome for hungry men returning from a hard day's work in the fields. My mother used to cook it every Tuesday.

   4 medium-sized potatoes, cut into cubes
   1 small carton of tomato passata
   250g small pasta tubes or shells
   1 small onion, thinly sliced
   1 clove of garlic, chopped
   salt, pepper
   2 tbsp olive oil
   4 tbsp grated parmesan cheese

In a deep pan, sauté the onion and garlic in the olive oil until they turn golden, add the cubed potatoes and the passata and cover with water and season. Boil gently for about 20 minutes.
Now add the pasta and cook until you feel it's ready. Before serving, sprinkle with parmesan and a drizzle of good olive oil.

A vivacious glass of Locorotondo would be superb.

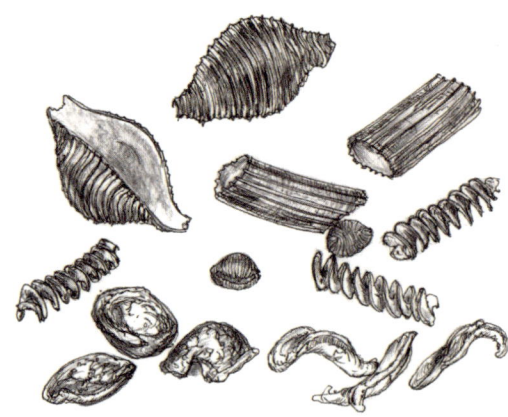

Pasta e cavolo
Pasta and cabbage

1 small cabbage (or cauliflower)
3 tbsp olive oil
400g big pasta shells
1 or 2 cloves of garlic, chopped
2 slices of stale white bread cut into cubes (croutons)
1 small piece of chilli

Put the chopped cabbage into a pan with plenty of salted water, bring to the boil. Cook for 15 minutes then add the pasta. Meanwhile, fry the croutons, chilli and the garlic in hot olive oil. As soon as the pasta is cooked, drain and add to the hot croutons and oil. Serve immediately with plenty of freshly ground pepper.

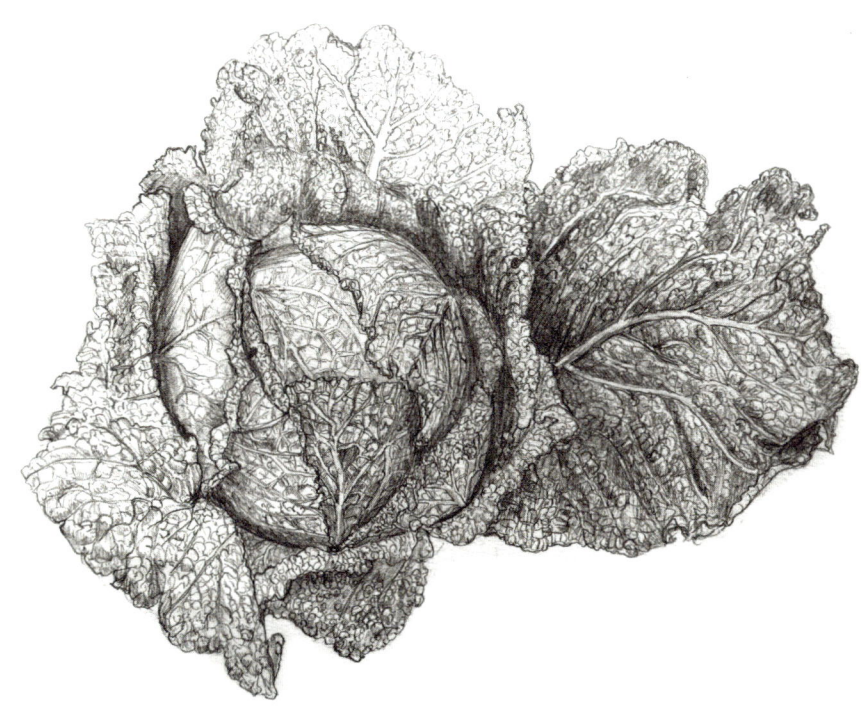

Cime di rape stufate
Braised turnip tops (or broccoli)

This is one of those simple, memorable dishes that evoke the essence of Puglia: the freshest turnip tops are stewed until soft in their juices with the addition of 1 bay leaf and 1 garlic clove, salt and pepper. Serve with a drizzle of olive oil, a few drops of lemon juice and a chunk of bread. Simple and heart warming.

Spuma di patate
Potato flan or cake

    1kg potatoes
    3 eggs
    5 tbsp parmesan
    50g sliced mortadella
    2 tbsp breadcrumbs
    20g butter
    a little grated nutmeg
    4 tbsp milk
    salt, pepper

Peel the potatoes and cut them into four. Boil and mash.
Add the parmesan, eggs, milk, nutmeg, salt and pepper.
In a greased oven dish, add one layer of the potato mixture, then the chopped mortadella and finally another layer of the potato mixture. Cover with breadcrumbs and knobs of butter and bake in a hot oven (200°C/gas mark 6) for half an hour or until it looks stupendously puffy and golden.
This dish is excellent served hot or cold and ideal for picnics.

Enjoy an honest bottle of Locorotondo with this.

Pasta e ceci
Pasta and chickpeas

A warming and delicious winter soup.

> 200g chickpeas soaked overnight with a teaspoon of bicarbonate
> 3 tbsp tomato pulp
> 200g pasta (cavatelli is the most authentic for this dish)
> a stick of celery
> 2 garlic cloves
> 2 bay leaves
> 1 sprig rosemary
> ½ chilli
> 3 tbsp extra virgin olive oil

Cook the pre-soaked chickpeas gently for about two hours in plenty of water, together with the bay leaves, garlic and celery, until they are soft. Add salt after an hour. When cooked add the tomato pulp, chilli, rosemary and pasta to the pan with more boiling water if needed. Simmer until the pasta is cooked.
Serve piping hot, adding some pepper and olive oil if you wish.

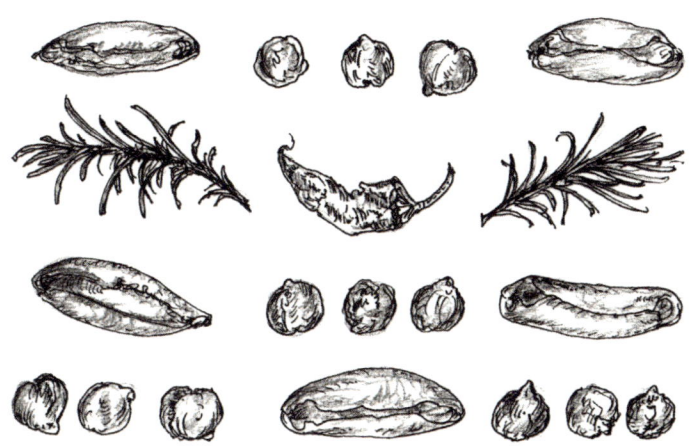

Braciole al ragu
Rolled beef parcels

This dish, also called *involtini* is a speciality in the whole of Puglia. I remember as a child being woken on Sunday mornings by the aroma of ragu which permeated all around our house. I could not wait for lunchtime to arrive! This is a tradition captured so well by the great playwright Eduardo De Filippo in his play *Saturday, Sunday, Monday*.

> 500g orecchiette or maccheroni
> 1kg beef topside, cut into thin slices (allow 1 or 2 per person)
> 100g pecorino cheese, grated
> 4 cloves of garlic, crushed
> 100g streaky bacon, chopped
> 1 onion, finely chopped
> a bunch of parsley, chopped
> 1kg peeled and chopped tomatoes or 1 large tin of plum tomatoes
> 1 carton tomato passata
> glass red or dry white wine
> 3 tbsp olive oil, salt and pepper
> 100g parmesan cheese, grated

Season the beef slices and flatten so they are nice and thin. Mix together the grated pecorino, 3 crushed garlic cloves and parsley, and spread the mixture on the beef slices. Add the chopped bacon, roll into small parcels and tie with thread. Heat the olive oil in a deep pan and fry the sliced onion and remaining garlic gently for a minute. Add the rolls, turning them until they are nicely brown all over. Add the wine and let it evaporate. Now add the tomatoes, passata, salt and pepper.

Simmer, covered, on a low heat for two hours watching to make sure they do not burn. If necessary, add more water to keep the meat covered. Before serving, remove the thread from the parcels.

Serve the sauce spooned over the *primo piatto* (i.e. orecchiette or maccheroni), adding a generous helping of *parmigiano*. The meat rolls are served as a *secondo piatto* and are best accompanied by a refreshing green salad.

Accompany with a glass of robust Primitivo.

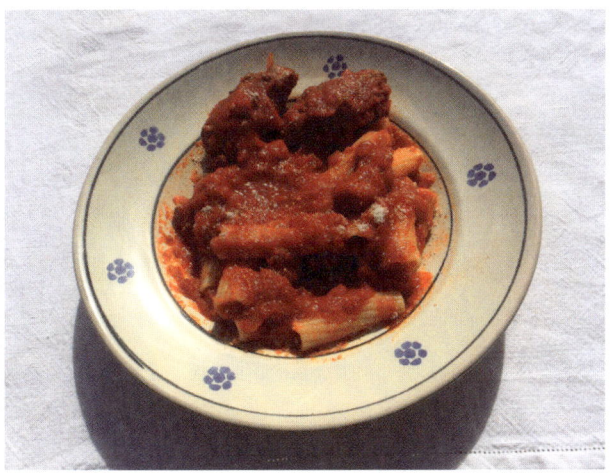

Polpette fritte e al sugo (e pasta a piacere)
Fried meatballs with tomato sauce and optional pasta

My children, Elisa and Simon, used to devour these on Thursdays when they came back from swimming, and now my grandchildren love polpette too. They are amazingly delicious, with or without the sauce.

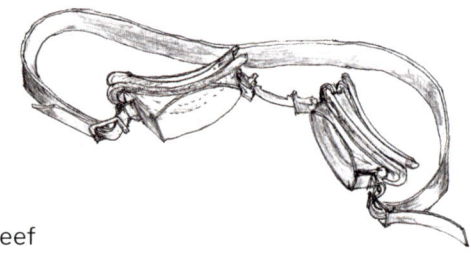

For the polpette:
- 400g best minced beef
- 1 egg
- 1 big clove of garlic, finely chopped
- 1 tbsp finely chopped parsley
- ½ tsp grated nutmeg
- 3 tbsp grated parmesan
- 2 slices white bread with crust removed, moistened in a little milk
- 6 tbsp white breadcrumbs
- 4 tbsp olive oil and 4 tbsp sunflower oil
- salt, pepper
- 5 tbsp grated parmesan

Put the meat in a bowl with all the other ingredients *except the breadcrumbs!* Take small pinches of the mixture and make little flattened balls. Roll in the breadcrumbs until covered.

Pour the two oils into a frying pan and, when really hot, fry the polpette, turning once or twice: they must be lovely and golden brown. Drain on kitchen paper.

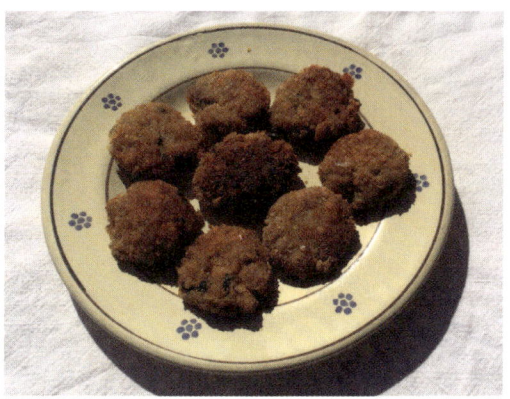

For the tomato sauce:
Fry one finely sliced onion in olive oil until golden. Add a large tin of peeled tomatoes, a small carton of passata, salt and pepper. Cook gently for about half an hour, adding some of the cooked polpette to the sauce for the last 10 minutes.
When ready, serve with some penne or maccheroni topped with the sauce, the polpette and some grated parmesan.

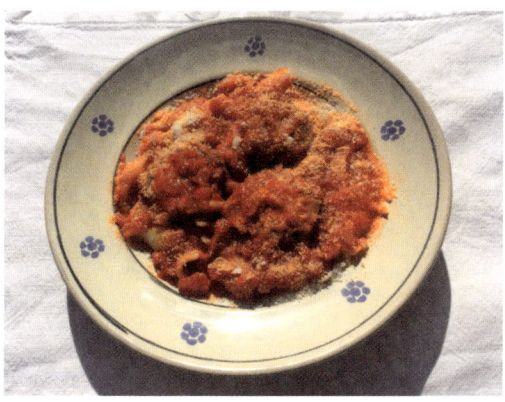

Melograno

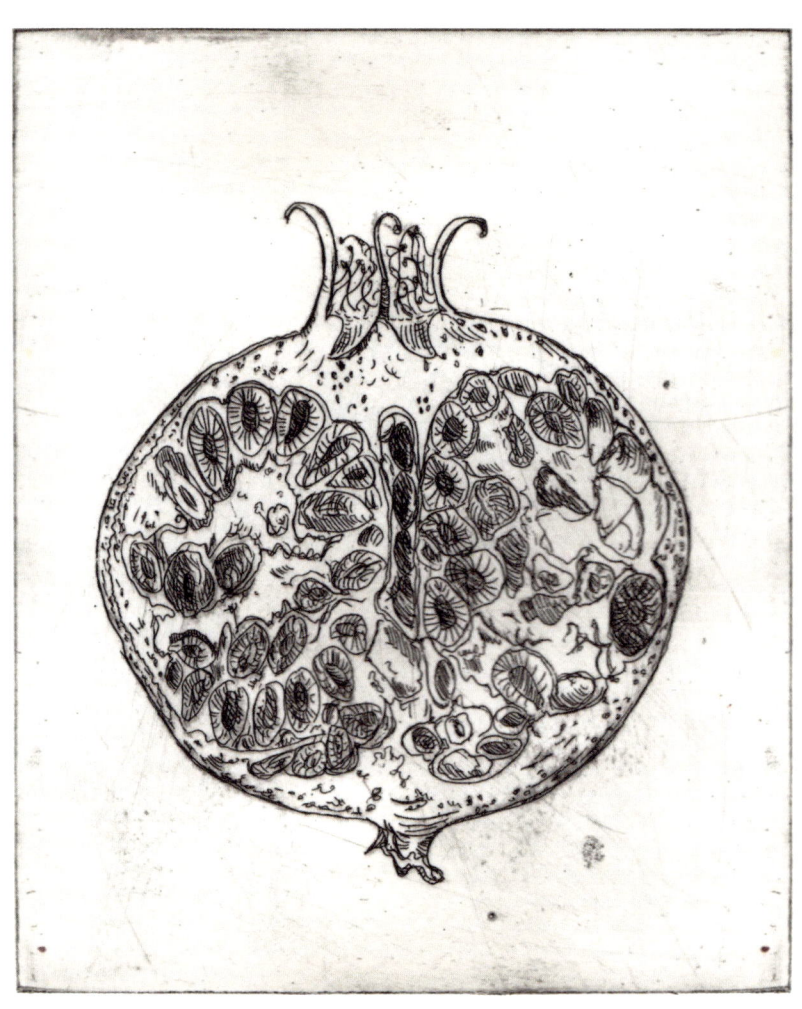

Pomegranate

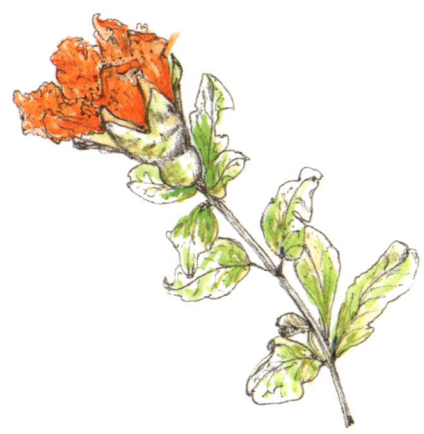

Throughout autumn and winter, scarlet pomegranates and bright orange loquats hang like vivid early Christmas baubles from bare trees, catching the low sunlight.

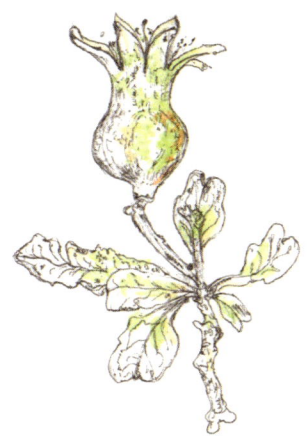

Pomegranates grow in abundance in Puglia and are much loved and respected not only for their ancient history, but also for their healthy antioxidant qualities. A glass of pomegranate juice a day will help fight Alzheimer's, cancer, heart disease and much more…

Christmas

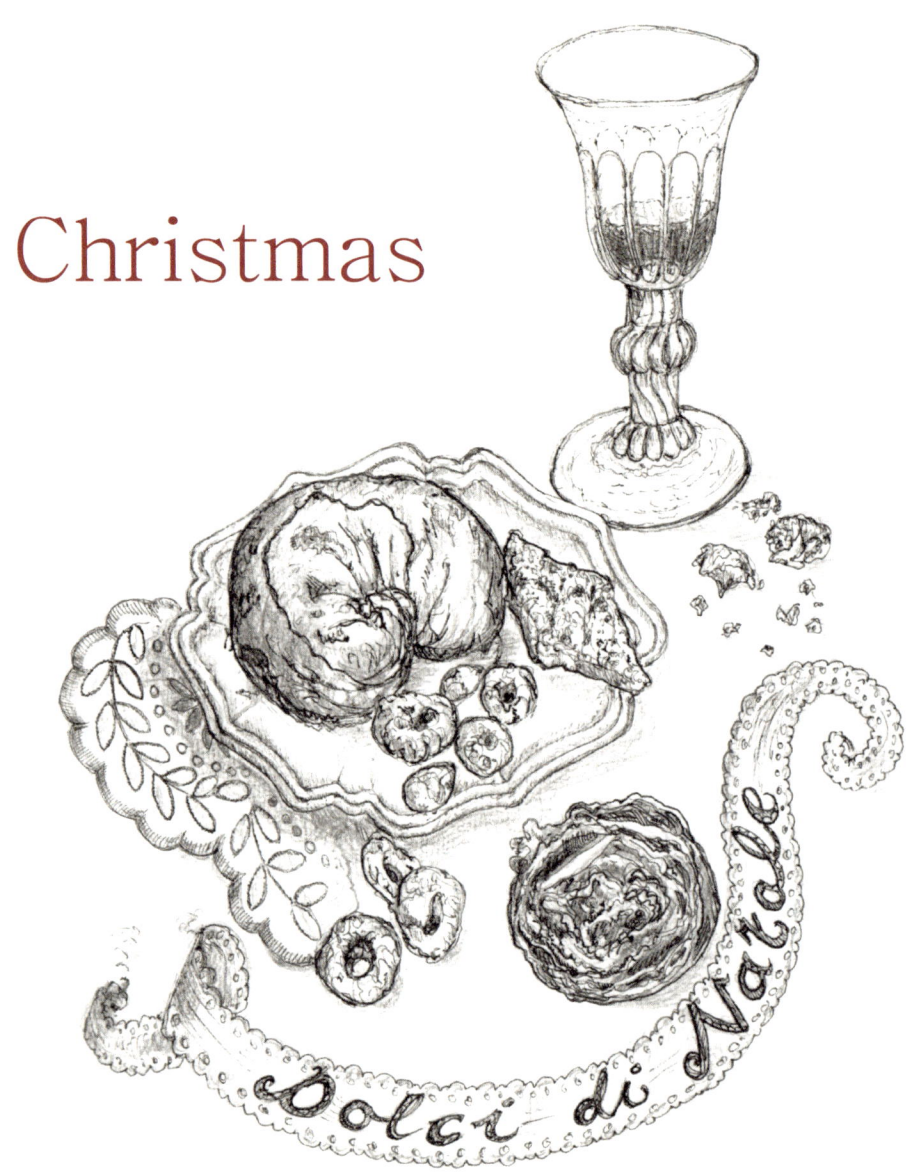

'It is through celebration that we become part of what we perceive.'
Confucius

Sfogliatelle
Stuffed pastries

For the pastry:
- 1kg flour
- 2 eggs
- 200g sugar
- 100ml olive oil
- 100ml white wine

For the stuffing:
- 500g almonds, peeled, crushed and roasted
- 400g sugar
- vanilla pod
- zest of 2 lemons and 2 oranges
- 2 tbsp of quince or grape jam (marmalade will do)
- ¼ tsp cinnamon
- small pieces of your favourite chocolate

Mix all the stuffing ingredients in a bowl.
For the base, mix the flour, sugar, oil and wine, and work to a smooth dough. Roll out until very thin and cut into strips measuring 15 x 10cm.
Add about a dessertspoonful of stuffing to each strip down the centre of the long side, fold over and after sealing the stuffing in make into a circular shape (or whatever shapes you wish).
Place on greaseproof paper on a tray and brush each with olive oil.
Bake at 200°C/gas mark 6 for 15 to 20 minutes.

Pesce · Fish

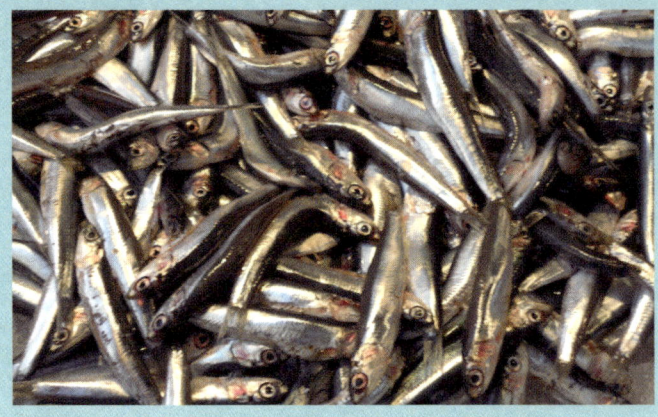

With 800 km of coastline, the importance of fish in the lives of the *Pugliesi* is no surprise. The fishermen stack their displays – *bancarelle di frutti di mare* – with an enormous variety of shellfish including oysters, scallops, mussels, clams, sea urchins (*ricci*), sea dates and razor shells. Buying and eating seafood on the spot is one of our greatest pleasures.

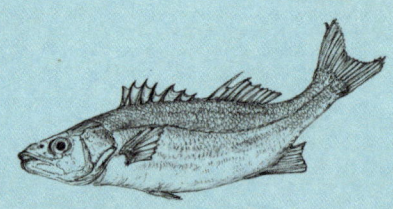

In the same way as we now buy ice cream, fish vendors used to come by on the beach selling shellfish by the dozen. My mother would buy twenty four fresh *cozze* (mussels) for ten *lire*, and they would be devoured immediately, usually drenched in lemon juice. This was the moment we children were encouraged to gather round for our first taste of the sea.

The passion for fresh seafood means that you will always see men digging up sea-snails at the water's edge, or prising minute limpets off the rocks. As for sea urchins, we can't ever have enough of them. The *ricci* bars along the Salento coast will serve fifty at a time as an aperitif with a lovely glass of their own bianco. At one memorable lunch by the sea, three of us managed to eat nearly three hundred in one sitting!

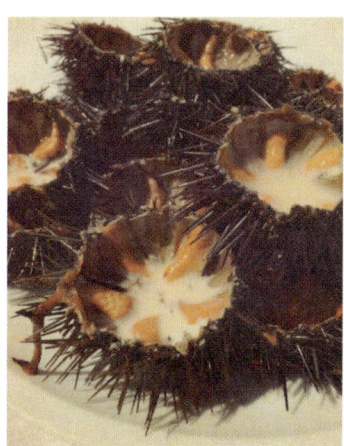
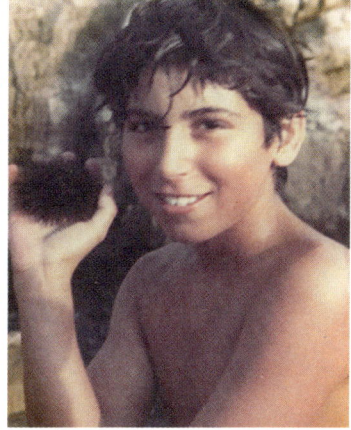

Sea urchins: Neptune's caviar

Tiella alla barese
Baked rice with mussels

500g mussels
300g arborio rice
2 medium onions, finely sliced
500g ripe cherry tomatoes
500g potatoes, peeled and sliced
4 tbsp finely chopped parsley
2 cloves of garlic, peeled and crushed
2 tbsp grated pecorino cheese
3-4 tbsp extra virgin olive oil
salt, pepper

Scrub and wash the mussels in several changes of water. Discard any that are open, and steam for about three or four minutes in a covered pan in a little boiling water. Take two thirds of them and remove the top empty shells (set aside the rest).

In an oiled clay pot, alternate a layer of onions and tomatoes, sprinkled with some parsley and garlic, with a layer of potatoes (half the total quantity). On top, add the half shelled mussels and their juices followed by the rice. Add another layer of garlic, parsley and tomatoes, sprinkle with olive oil, salt and pepper and then the final layer of potatoes. Top with grated pecorino and a few chopped tomatoes. Add water around the edge (about 250 ml), sprinkle over the breadcrumbs and finish with an abundant drizzle of extra virgin olive oil. Season and bake at 180°C/gas mark 4 for about 45 minutes, or until the rice is cooked.

To serve, lay the remaining 150g of mussels (in half of their shells) on top and return the pot to the oven for a few more minutes.
In summer a couple of thinly sliced courgettes can be added in between the layers.

With this dish indulge in a good bottle of wine of your choice.

Cozze alla leccese
Mussels with oil, lemon and parsley

One of a dozen ways of preparing this favourite shellfish. There is no fish dish simpler than this.

>   1kg mussels
>   1 lemon, squeezed
>   3 tbsp olive oil
>   a bunch of finely chopped parsley
>   salt, pepper

In a bowl mix the lemon juice, olive oil, parsley, salt and pepper.

Scrub the mussels and wash in several changes of water. Discard any which are broken or open. Put the mussels in a pan, add a little water, cover and steam until they open (about 3 or 4 minutes). When ready, remove the top part of the shell. Place on serving plates and pour a little of the dressing onto each shell.

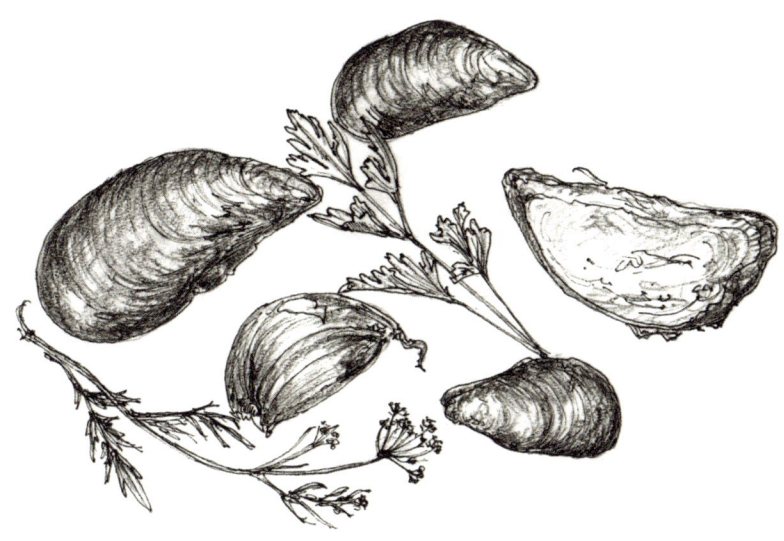

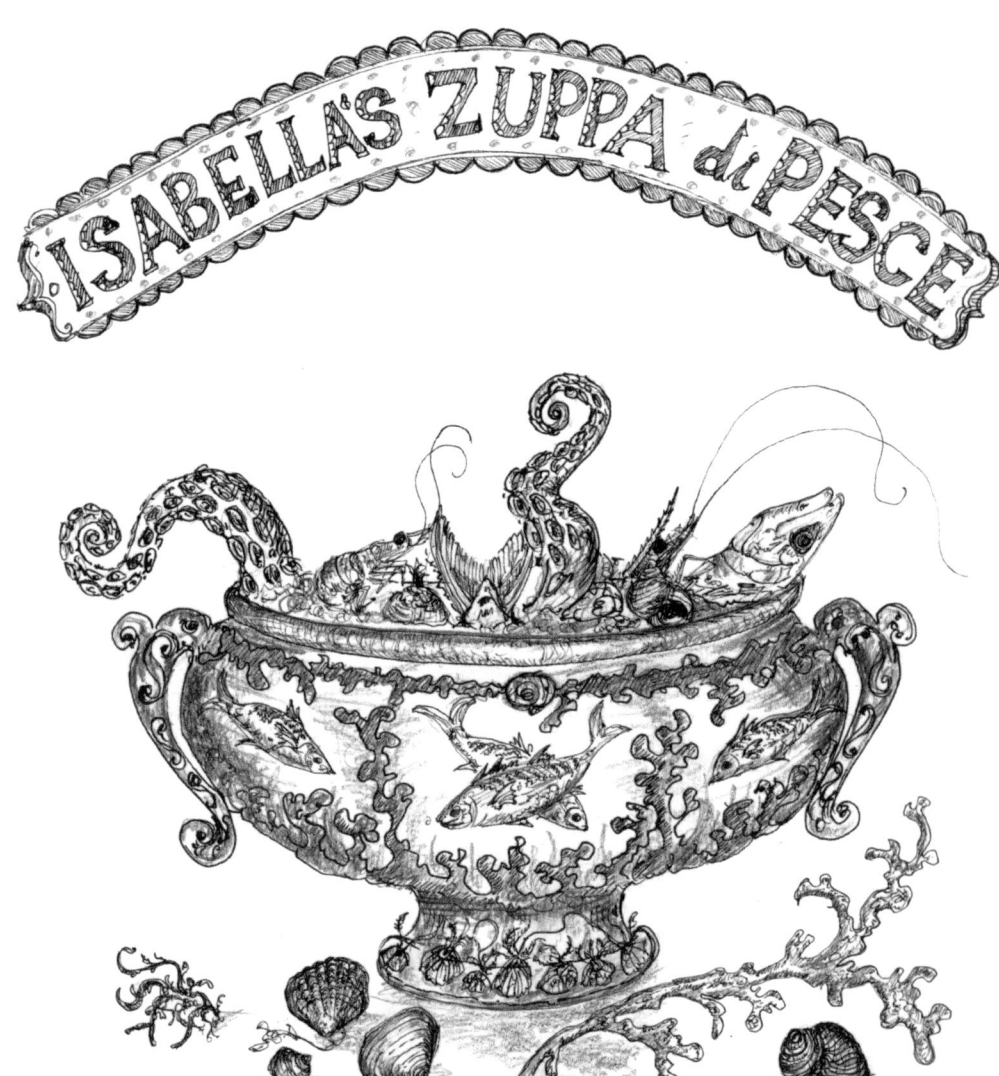

Isabella's zuppa di pesce
Isabella's fish soup

My mother used to make this every Friday during the summer. The local catch would include so many varieties of fish. Most were small and some were quite bony, but they were full of flavour. Larger fish can be cut into smaller pieces.

Tomato base:
- 2-3 cloves of garlic, crushed
- 1 onion, finely sliced
- 1 chilli, chopped, or a pinch of red pepper flakes
- 1 green pepper, cut into quarters (optional)
- 2 tbsp extra virgin olive oil
- 200g ripe tomatoes
- salt and pepper,
- a splash of white wine, parsley

Seafood:
- An assortment of cephalopod molluscs, such as squid, baby cuttlefish or octopus, cut into bite-sized pieces.
- A variety of firm-fleshed fish of your choice, such as monkfish, *scorfano* (scorpion fish), or *triglie* (red mullet), cut into large chunks.
- Any combination of shrimp, crayfish, clams and mussels

Sauté the crushed garlic cloves and onion in plenty of olive oil. When the garlic begins to give off its aroma and is just barely beginning to brown, add the tomato – ideally the pulp of fresh, perfectly ripe San Marzano tomatoes – and the chilli pepper. Season with salt and pepper, add finely chopped parsley and simmer for about 10 minutes, or until the mixture begins to reduce and reach a saucy consistency. Add a splash of white wine. Now add your seafood, starting with the varieties that take the longest to cook, such as squid and octopus. After 10 minutes or so check seasoning and, if satisfied, serve immediately.

We used to mop up the wonderful juices with morsels of bread. We Italians call this *'fare la scarpetta'* (polish the shoe).

Alici in tortiera
Baked anchovies

    600g fresh anchovies, or fresh sardines
    2 cloves of garlic, finely chopped
    1 bunch chopped parsley
    1 tbsp capers
    3 tbsp breadcrumbs
    2 or 3 tbsp extra virgin olive oil
    salt and pepper

Bone and wash the anchovies or sardines. Flatten each fish with the palm of your hand. Grease a baking pan, line its base with a layer of anchovies skin side down and season them with all the ingredients, finishing with the breadcrumbs. Drizzle with olive oil, salt and pepper, and bake in a hot oven for 5 to 10 minutes or until the surface turns golden. Serve hot or cold.

Gravina bianco, with its delicate and fresh taste would be lovely with this dish.

Orata alla pugliese
Sea bream, Pugliese style

You can use sea bream or any similar fish.

   a large sea bream (approx. 800g)
   500g potatoes
   50g pecorino
   a generous amount of chopped parsley
   2 cloves of finely chopped garlic
   olive oil
   salt and pepper
   1 tbsp breadcrumbs

Oil the bottom of an oven dish, add half the potatoes, parsley, pecorino and garlic. Place the fish on top, and cover with the remaining potatoes, herbs and cheese. Top with a handful of breadcrumbs and sprinkle with olive oil, salt and pepper.
Place in a hot oven (200°C/gas mark 6) for about 40 minutes. Shake the dish during cooking to avoid the potatoes sticking to the bottom of the pan.

Don't forget a good bottle of Fiano with this!

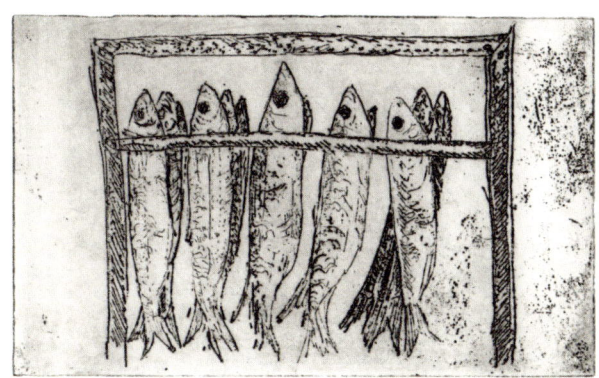

Polpi in umido
Stewed octopus

The octopus, 'Old no-bones the polyp' as Hesiod called it, was a powerful fertility symbol in Mycenaean times. Pugliesi men love catching these alarming creatures, then bashing them against the rocks to soften them. Their wives will complete the labour by cooking them for the family lunch.

500g octopus
300g ripe tomatoes, chopped
2 cloves of garlic, chopped
3 tbsp extra virgin olive oil
large glass of dry red wine
bunch of parsley, finely chopped
3 tbsp extra virgin olive oil
1 tsp sugar
salt, pepper

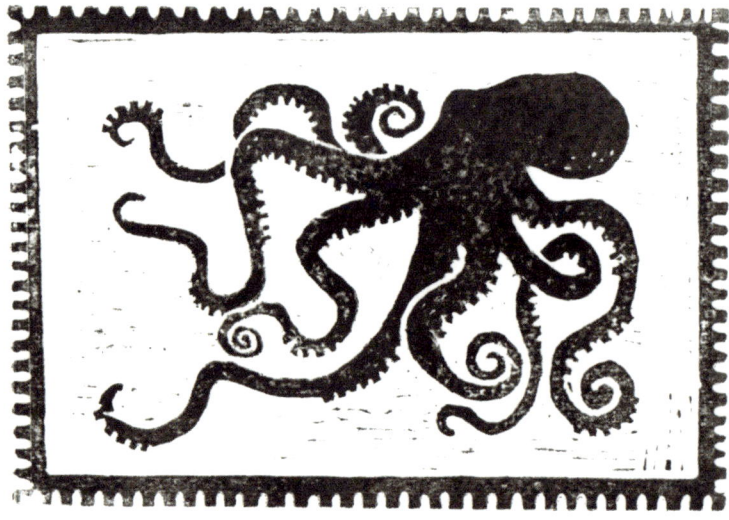

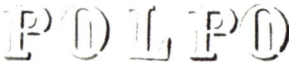

Blanch for a couple of minutes in boiling water to get rid of the scum that forms. Cut into pieces and fry lightly in hot oil, turning them over once. Add garlic until golden, then add the wine, tomatoes, salt, pepper and a little sugar.

Cover with water and simmer until tender – about 20 minutes for a baby octopus and 50 minutes for a medium one. Sprinkle with chopped parsley and serve immediately. A chunk of rustic bread is ideal for mopping up the juices.

Note: Octopus is now almost always sold already cleaned. If not, turn the body inside out, pull away and discard the entrails, cut out the eyes and gristle with a sharp knife, and clean thoroughly under cold running water.

Spigola al forno
Baked sea bass

Sea bass is the most noble fish and one of our absolute favourites. We appreciate it so much that only the minimum treatment is tolerated.

>   sea bass weighing about 1kg
>   3-4 tbsp extra virgin olive oil
>   salt, pepper

Scale, wash and gut the fish. Sprinkle lightly with salt inside and out, and rub with olive oil. Wrap loosely in a large sheet of silver foil twisting the edges together.
Cook (220°C/gas mark 7) for 30-45 minutes.
Serve with wedges of lemon and a drizzle of olive oil.

Un po' di questo e quello

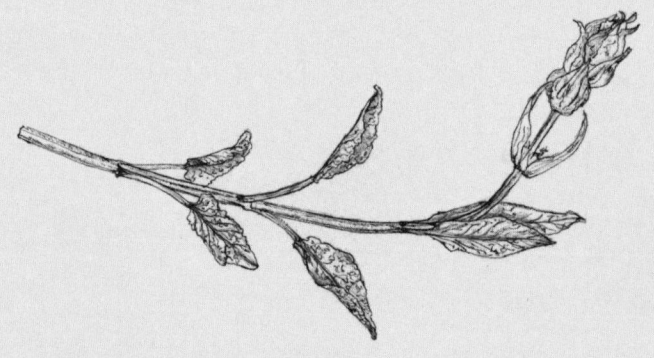

A bit of this and that

Pane · Bread

Bread plays a central role in Pugliese cuisine, and Pane di Altamura is the best: a wonderful sourdough bread made with durum wheat, water and salt, shaped into enormous loaves.

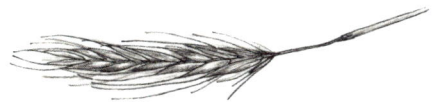

Bread is never thrown away. Hard bread is used for making breadcrumbs and the delightful polpette di pane (bread balls). This is how you make them:

Mix 200g stale bread (softened with a little milk), 2 eggs, 80g parmigiano or pecorino cheese, 1 clove of chopped garlic, and 1 tbsp finely chopped parsley. The consistency should be soft but not mushy. Amalgamate all and form little balls. Fry in very hot olive oil until golden. Eat immediately.

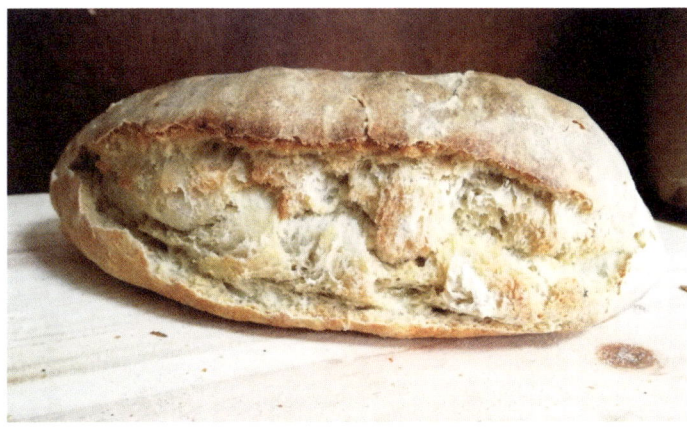

Sale!   Salt!

Cooking fish NEEDS salt. It is one of those magic ingredients – too little and the food tastes insipid, too much and what you have prepared is inedible. The right amount brings out the true flavour of all ingredients. My advice: if in doubt, add a pinch!

My feelings are summed up in this short extract from Pablo Neruda's poem *'Ode to Salt'*

.....taste imparts to every seasoned

dish your ocean essence;

and then on every table

in the world,

salt,

we see you piquant

powder

sprinkling

vital light

upon

our food

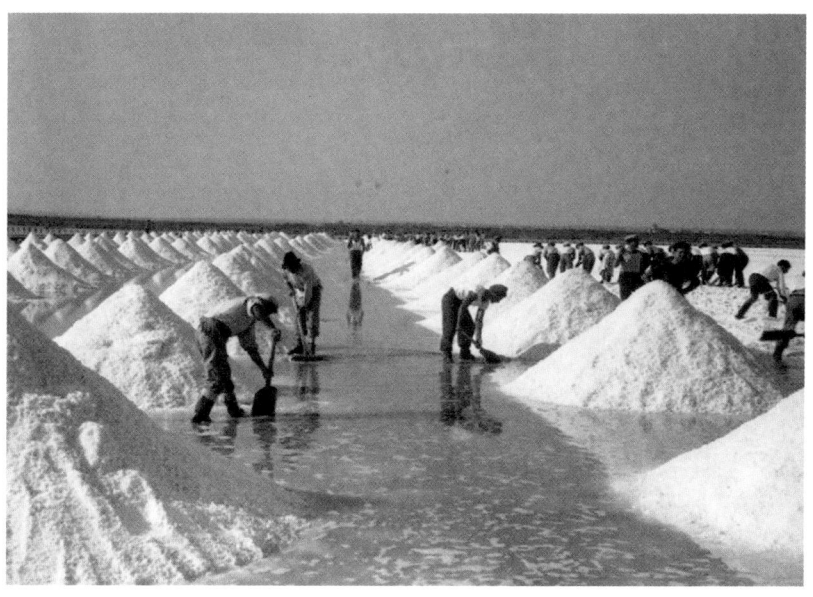

*Le Saline of Margherita di Savoia
The 'mountains' of salt near Trinitapoli, my birthplace*

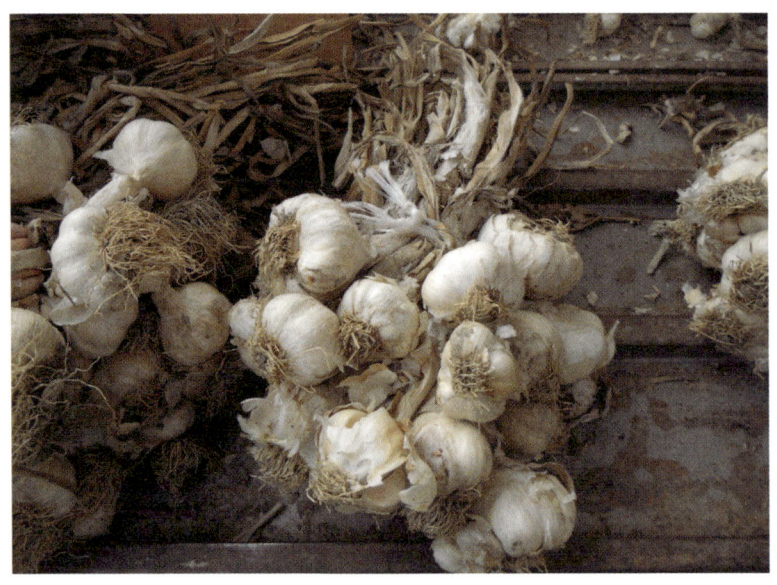

'And I must tell you that I have had a whole field of garlic planted for your benefit, so that when you come we may be able to have plenty of your favourite dishes.'
Beatrice d'Este, writing from a hunting lodge in the Ticino
to her sister in Mantua, in 1491

'Do not eat garlic or onions; for their smell will reveal that you are a peasant.'
Cervantes, Don Quixote

Aglio · Garlic

Garlic is a crucial ingredient for most of our recipes: without it our orecchiette e cime di rape and many other dishes would be tasteless and bland.

I urge you to crush your cloves liberally and add to the burning oil until it becomes the gold that spices up whatever it touches.

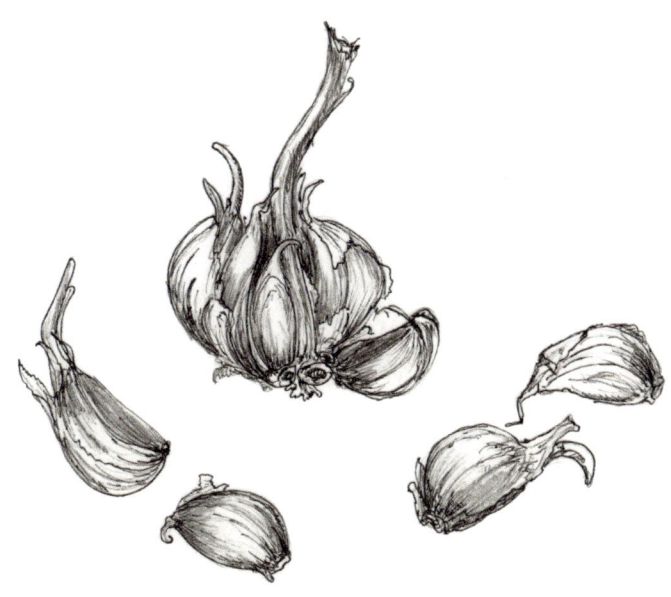

Fico d'India • Prickly pear

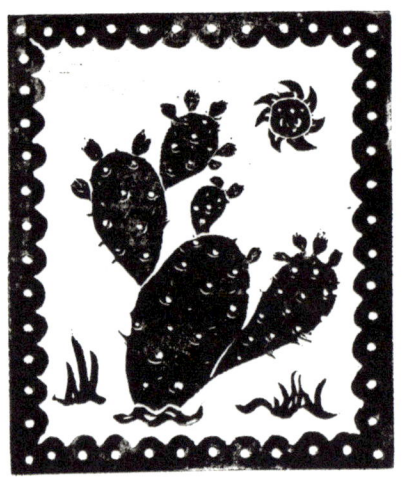

My uncle Pantaleo found this fruit irresistible. He was capable of devouring a plateful of them whilst warning us children of the consequences: *"ti fanno male pima quando li cogli, poi quando li mangi e qualche ora dopo!"* (you suffer three times: first when picking them, then when eating them, then afterwards!)

Fichi d'India are native to Mexico but have become naturalised in the Mediterranean, where their impenetrable thickets are often used to mark boundary lines.

In late summer, markets all over Puglia are laden with these extraordinary, colourful fruit. They taste better when orange-red, in the early morning, after rain. If eaten in moderation, they can help with cholesterol, obesity and... a hangover!

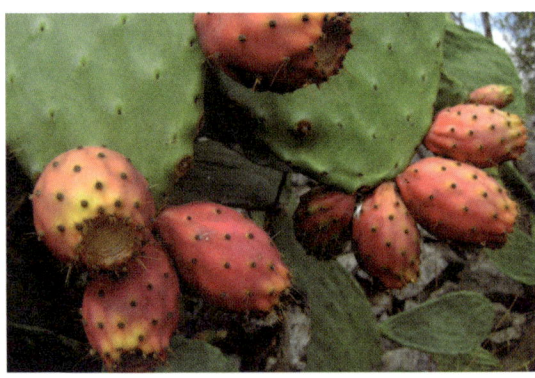

Prickly pears at Pascarosa

Rosmarino · Rosemary

A sudden heavy shower in Summer is enough to reveal its presence through the Mediterranea scrub, its smell stronger than any other shrub. Much appreciated by all the ancient civilisations for its innumerable properties and its uses.

The Egyptians used it to cure stomach and liver diseases.
Greeks used it as incense to sacrifices to the gods.
Romans used the herb for strengthening the memory.
In Middle Ages it was planted in monasteries to drive out evil spirits and witches.

We now use it to enhance the flavour of a good piece of lamb.

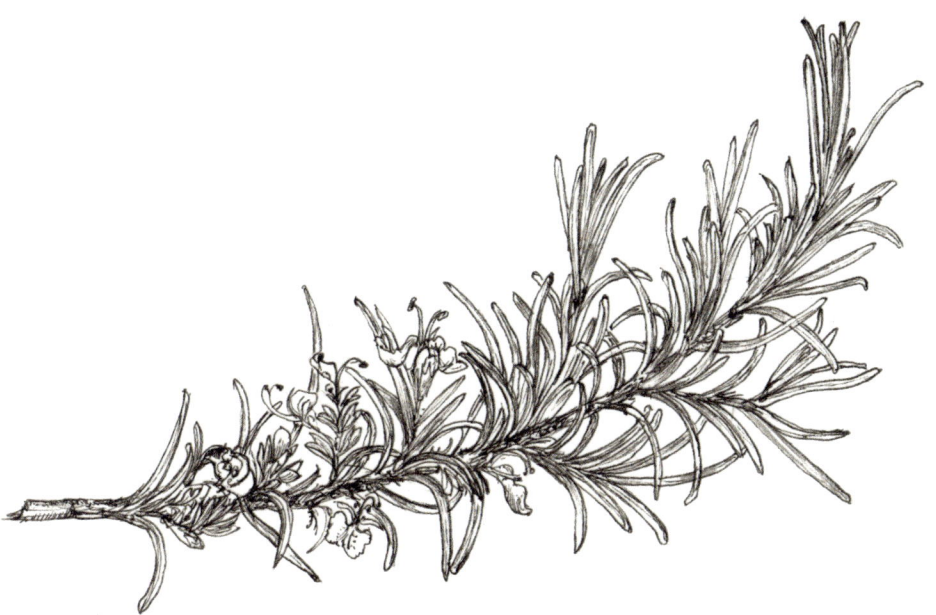

rosemarinus officinalis

LIQUORI

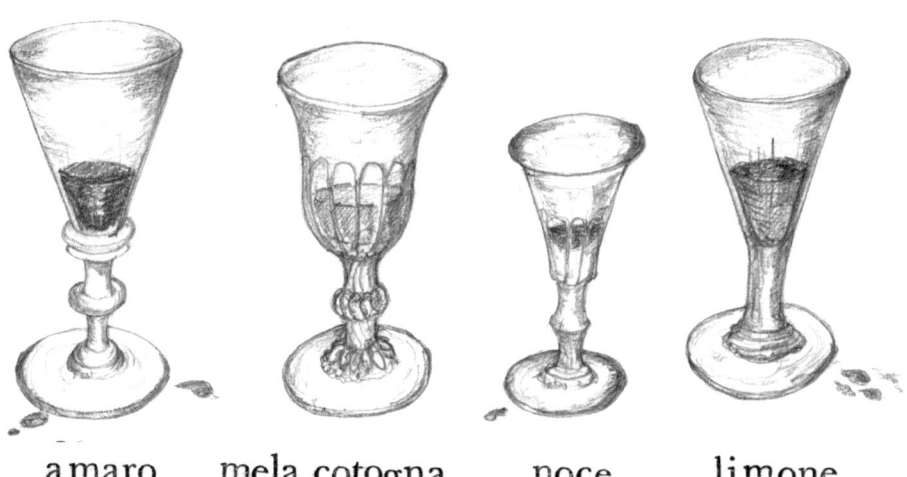

amaro   mela cotogna   noce   limone

Rosoli · Liquori · Liqueurs

Gradisci un goccio di rosolio?

Would you like a drop of liqueur? Usually asked of guests coming to share a special meal – there is nothing better or more satisfying than a few gulps of the sugary (often fiery) concoctions made with love and kept for those special occasions.

Whenever my mother came to London, she used to smuggle in her bag a huge bottle of pure alcohol which she would transform into a variety of colourful rosoli: strega, caffe' or amaretto, my favourites.

These liqueurs are quite easy to make but they are almost impossible to find in the UK: you need 100% pure alcohol. However, I have discovered that you can buy a Polish bottle (95%) for £30!

Vino è Vino

In her later years, when *enoteche* (wine shops) started selling good and often famous wines from all over Italy, my mother used to object fiercely to the idea of buying from them, saying that we must drink the wine made by our cousins – even though this sometimes had dubious results… She was very critical of my English musician husband, who used to buy what she thought were extortionately expensive bottles from the enoteca.
Her words: **'*ma vino è vino!*'** ('but wine is wine!').

In fact, for many Pugliesi, wine is still a simple everyday commodity, especially for those who make their own. It is seen as something to be drunk, not fussed over. Of course there is also the world of famous wines from the best growing areas such as Brunello, Barolo, or the wonderful Fiano and Falanghina from Campania. But these are seen as wines to be appreciated only by people who can afford their sometimes prohibitive prices.

My favourite *vini pugliesi*:

Red
Negroamaro, Primitivo, Salice Salentino, Aglianico
and the historic Susumaniello to drink with robust dishes.

White
Fiano Puglia, Castel del Monte, Locorotondo, Verdeca
and Gravina to enjoy with fish and delicate dishes.

Rosé
I never drink them.

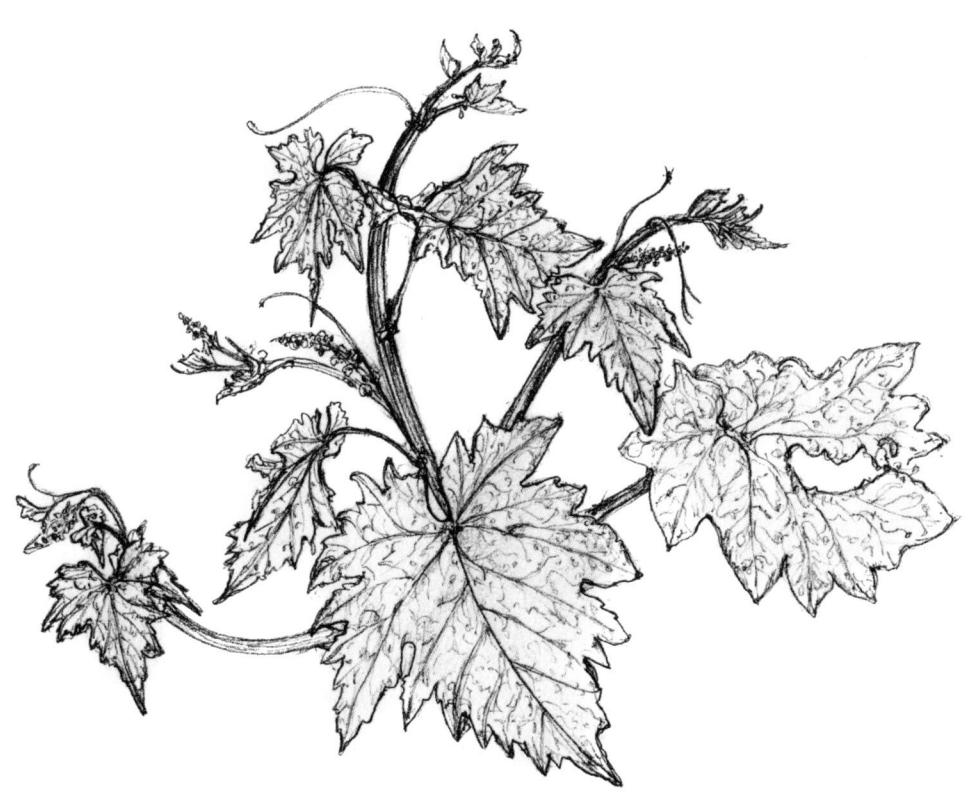

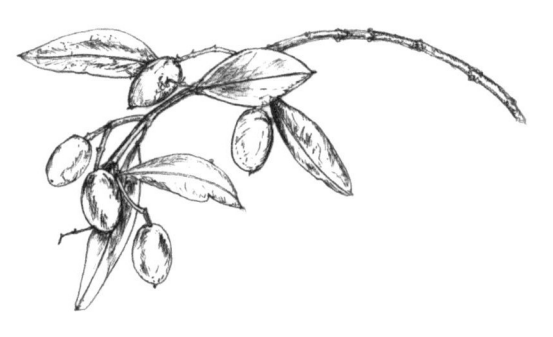

Recipes in page order

Antipasti • Starters   16

    melanzane alla griglia 17
    fiori di zucchine fritti 18
    zucchine fritte 18
    cozze arraganate 19
    i sott'aceti *preserved vegetables* 20

Primavera • Spring   22

    erbe spontanee *edible weeds* 23
    cicorielle 23
    lambascioni 24
    asparago selvatico 27
    asparago selvatico con uova 27
    pasta primavera con fagiolini e pomodoro 28
    peperoni friggitelli fritti 29
    pasta con fave e piselli 30
    carciofi *artichokes* 31
    carciofi fritti 32
    carciofi ripieni col sugo e pasta 33
    agnello con patate 34
    agnello al verdetto 35
    scarcella or 'scarcedda' 36

Estate • Summer 37

orecchiette con pomodoro e ricotta salata 38
spaghetti con pomodori al forno 39
pomodori ripieni 40
zucchine alla poveredda 41
minestra di zucchine 42
parmigiana di melanzane 43
peperoni arrosto con acciughe, capperi e aglio 44
cialdedda 44
mandorle *almonds* 47
marzapani 49
tarallini 49

Autunno • Autumn 50

about olive oil 52
olive fresche fritte 54
verdure *autumn and winter vegetables* 55
finocchi in insalata 56
finocchi con olio e parmigiano 58
insalata di puntarelle 59
zucca al forno con merluzzo 60
zucca alla ricotta forte 61
zuppa di cavolfiore 62
funghi *wild mushrooms* 63
funghi porcini trifolati 64
pollo con funghi porcini 65

Inverno • Winter 68

orecchiette con cime di rape 69
fave e cicoria 70
pasta e patate 72
pasta e cavolo 73
cime di rape stufate 74

spuma di patate 74
pasta e ceci 75
braciole al ragu 76
polpette fritte e al sugo e pasta 78
melograno *pomegranate* 81
sfogliatelle 83

Pesce • Fish   84

tiella alla barese 86
cozze alla leccese 87
Isabella's zuppa di pesce 89
alici in tortiera 90
orata alla pugliese 91
polpi in umido 92
spigola al forno 93

Un po' di questo e quello   94

pane 95
polpette di pane 95
sale 96
aglio 99
fico d'India 100
rosmarino 101
rosoli *liqueurs* 103
Vino è Vino 104

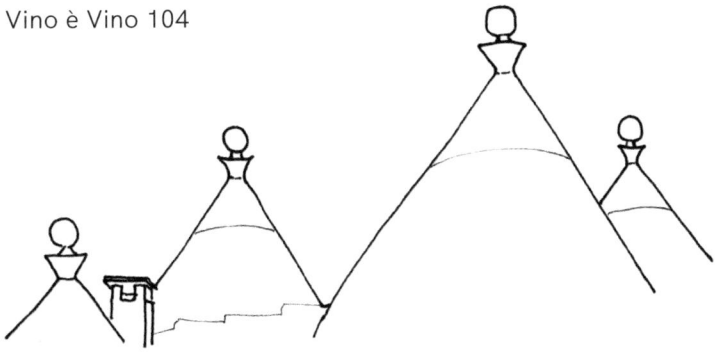

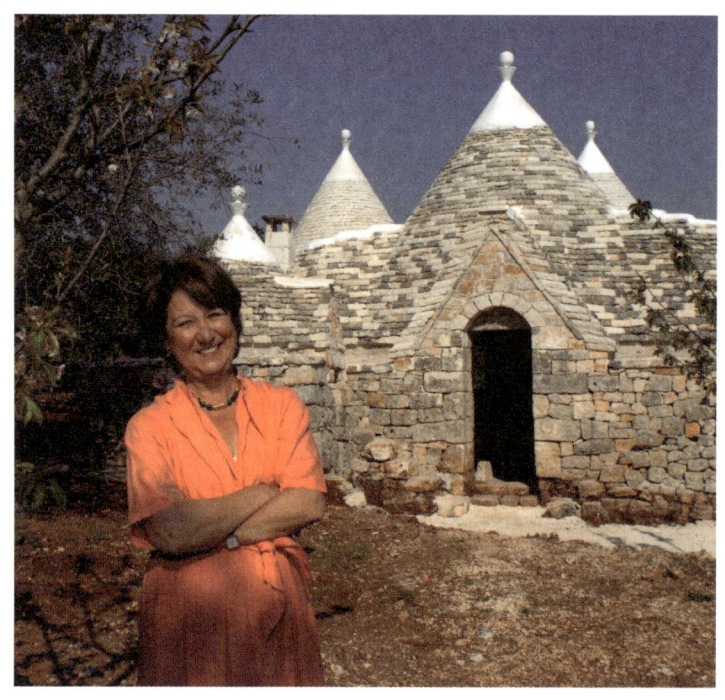

*We shall not cease from exploration
And the end of all our exploring
Will be to arrive where we started
And know the place for the first time.*

T. S. Eliot

Acknowledgements

My first big thank you goes to Emma Hobbins whose breathtakingly beautiful work I love and cherish. Without Emma, this book would have never been written. For precious advice and assistance my infinite thanks to Gaby Wine who read the first draft and encouraged me to continue with it. I'm indebted to Sarah Nettleton for editing the book, her exquisite attention to detail is amazing. Warm thanks to Benedict Cruft whose precious suggestions helped to make the recipes clear and accurate, and to Linde Hardaker and Frankie Hobbins for their invaluable contributions.

And last, but not least, thanks to my family, who have always cherished and loved the things I cook.

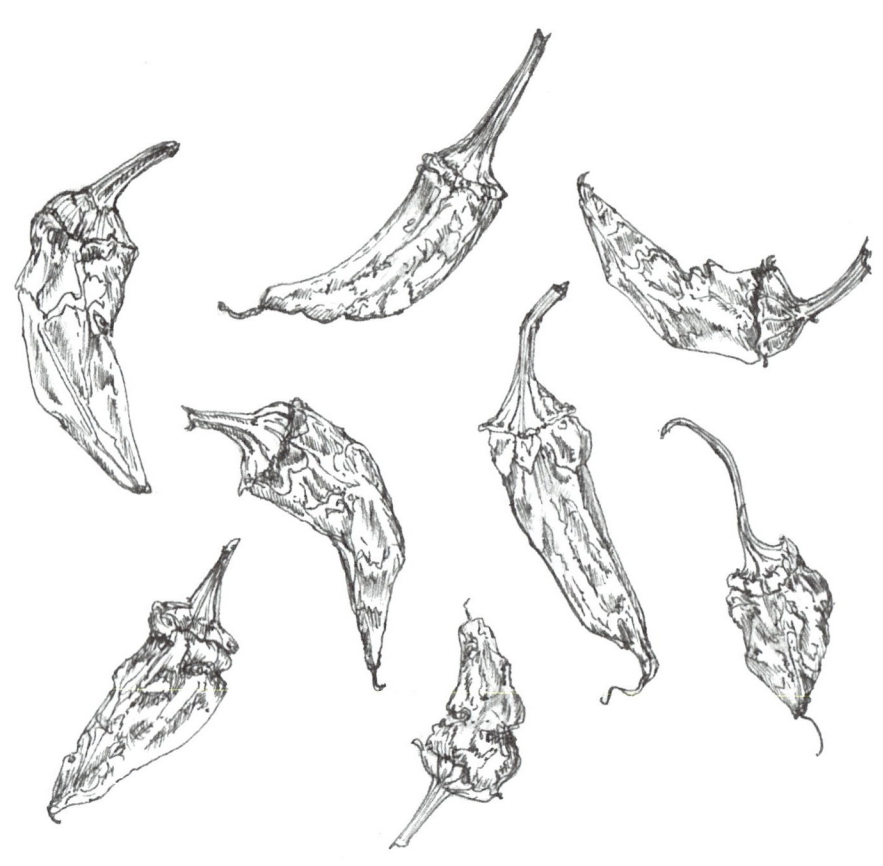

FINE

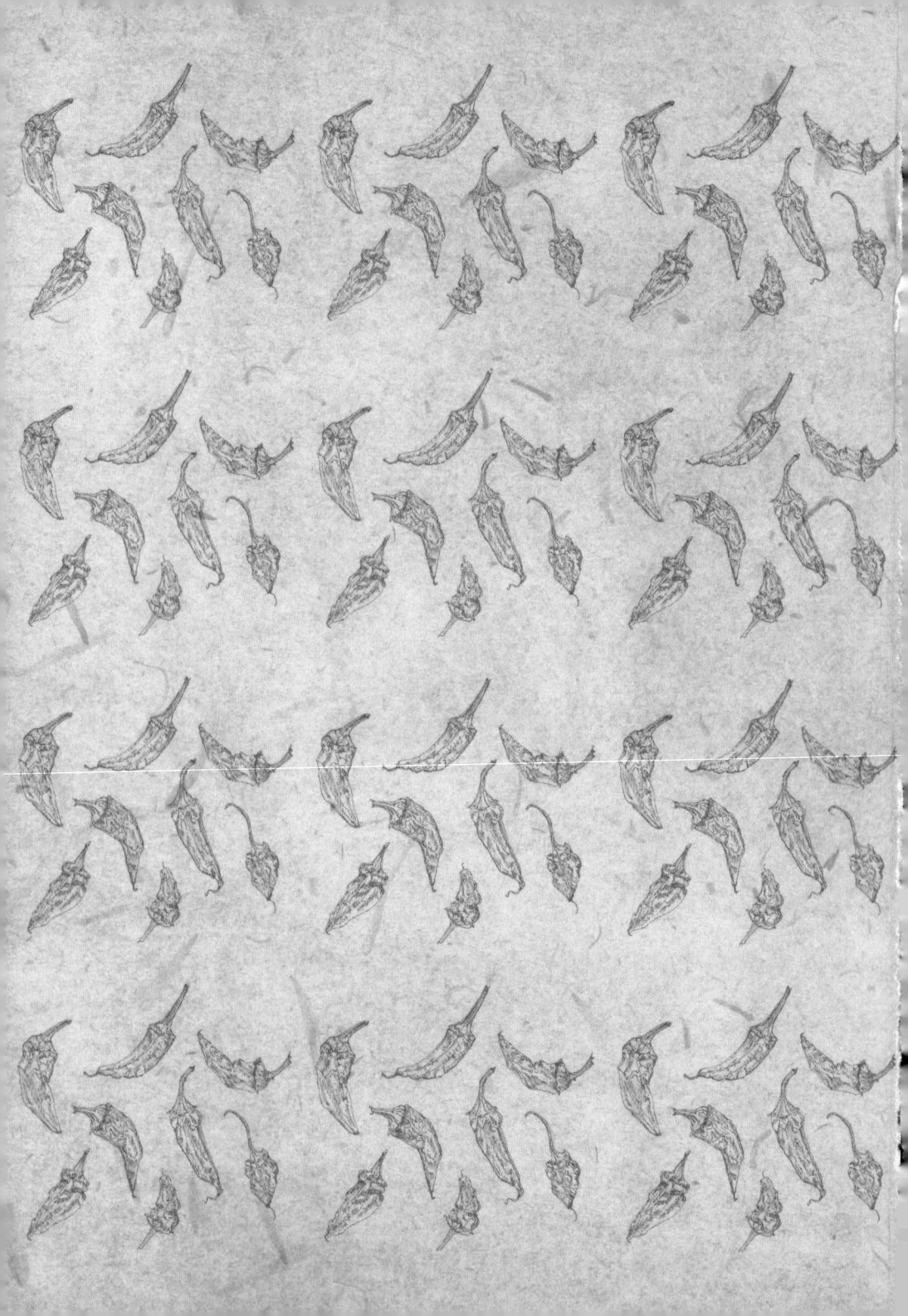